HAPPINESS

A Spiritual Awakening from the Inside Out

MATT MORRIS

Contents

Sections	v
Preface	vii
Introduction	xi
1. Personal Growth Questions	1
2. Relationship Questions	4
3. Fun Questions	6
4. Health Questions	8
5. Career Questions	10
6. Money Questions	12
7. Physical Location Questions	14
8. Master Questions for Elaboration and More Coaching Questions	16
Afterword	19
Preface	23
Introduction	27
9. Pieces of Your Identity	30
10. Letting Go Of Your Past	40
11. A New Perspective	52
12. Seeing Past The Wildflowers	74
13. A Brighter Future	86
14. Your New Gift	94
15. Perpetual Happiness	109
16. Scientific Studies Showing The Positive Effects Of Living In The Present Moment	118
17. Great Minds Think In The Present Moment	128
18. The Puzzle of The Present Moment	136
19. Q & A	144
Afterword	165
Section III. Positive Thinking is the Gateway to Happiness	167
Introduction	169

20. The Road to Positivity	171
21. Ways to a Stress-Free Life	176
22. Build Your Confidence	181
23. Bring On Positivity	187
24. Half Empty or Half Full?	192
Afterword	195
Section IV. Program Your Mind to Be Happy	197
Introduction	199
25. The Body, the Mind, and NLP	206
26. NLP in Business	226
Afterword	233
Section V. Set Goals to Reach Eternal Happiness	235
Introduction	237
27. How to Set an Unbreakable S.M.A.R.T. Goal!	244
28. Why You (and Everyone Else in the World) Needs S.M.A.R.T. Goals!	254
29. Staying Fired Up About Your Goals!	260
30. The Master Plan to S.M.A.R.T. Goals	266
31. Final Secrets That Only Few Know!	270
Afterword	277
Epilogue	278
Citations:	279

Sections

I. Powerful Questions to Discover What You Want

II. Be Happy NOW

III. Positive Thinking is the Gateway to Happiness

IV. Program Your Mind to Be Happy

V. Set Goals to Reach Eternal Happiness

Preface

If you ask 100 people what they want out of life, 70 out of 100 will say "to be happy", followed by "to be successful", "to serve my purpose", and "to be present or peace of mind". This book covers each of these topics in clear detail so that, taking you step-by-step to make massive transformations in your life.

Inside this book, you will discover what you truly want in life and how to get there. You will be shown how to enjoy each and every moment of your life so that you can stop stressing over things that have already happened and get rid of future worries in order to be fully present. You will discover your purpose and WHY you are here on this earth. You will learn how to get rid of that nasty voice inside your head that is constantly trying to sabotage your dreams. Last, but not least, you will find out how to set and achieve goals, whether it be success, to be in a wonderful relationship, or to feel more peaceful.

Each of these start from the inside out, and even though happiness is not a constant state, you will feel happiness light-years beyond any negative feelings such as depression, loneliness, and anger.

Section I. Powerful Questions to Discover What You Want

Introduction

The ability to ask powerful, open-ended questions is the most brilliant tool that we as humans can possess. They don't have to be earth-shattering or groundbreaking questions that leave listeners with their jaws hanging down to the ground, although they can be. More importantly, they need to be questions that will stimulate emotion to provoke "aha" moments, ones that lead the person in deep thought to inspire creativity, increase productivity, and blast glaring headlights on personal development.

Questions are the primary way to build a connection and develop lasting, meaningful relationships. They have brought peace into broken, confusing relationships; they have helped to solve life's most complicated problems; and, most importantly, they've brought a deeper level of understanding to humanity so that society as a whole can give and get more out of life.

The questions you are about to embark upon will be ones that will open many doors that you once believed were locked with ten deadbolts. They will be ones for you to use to guide others to find out what makes them tick—not like a time bomb, but instead like a grandfather clock on the wall waiting to strike midnight.

You will find that this section is divided into eight important categories so that you can immediately jump to any section as needed.

1

Personal Growth Questions

Coach, Listen, and Be Curious

Coaches have been recognized as leaders in creating powerful questions to evoke transformation. Coaches seek out to be leaders in both personal and business development. They get motivated to inspire, build, and connect with others, all of which begins with questions to determine what the other person *really* wants out of life.

Although questions are the primary focus of this section, it is important to understand that listening has equal importance in order for you to respond and create your own questions so that you can direct a conversation that will benefit the other person. Use the words a person uses to build other questions. For example, if a person says he doesn't like how things have changed, you can say, "What do you mean by change? Can you give me an example?" This leads to further, deeper conversation about more meaningful things.

Every day of life, we learn something new, whether we're talking with a friend about his newborn baby, watching the news about a massacre in Iraq, or realizing that we like to listen to the acoustic version of Led Zeppelin. We learn things about events in the world, ourselves, and facts about everyday life when we listen. Listening with our ears, observing things with our eyes, and following our intuition are simple examples of ways to listen and understand.

One more thing before we dive into the questions: the best questions come from being curious, non-judgmental, and open-minded. Allow yourself to be open to possibilities.

This section was created to provide ways for both you and the person you are speaking with to gain purpose and to understand oneself and others in deeper, more meaningful ways.

- What do you want in life?
- What is your dream?
- What is your purpose?
- What else?
- One month from now, where do you want to be? 3 months? 6 months? 1 year?
- What are you searching for?
- How will it feel to be there?
- What are you grateful for?
- Who do you want to be?
- What does that look like?
- What is important to you?
- Why is that important to you?
- Who do you admire, or what type of person do you look up to? If he/she could offer you advice, what would it be?
- What are 3 of the best qualities that you can bring to the situation?
- Tell me more.

Happiness

- Imagine how it would feel once you accomplish this.
- What is getting in the way of living the life you want to live?
- Why do you want to be like this?
- What will this bring you?
- What do you need to do to get there?
- What do you value in life?
- What's the challenge here?
- If you could do one thing every day, something that excites you to get out of bed every day, what would that be?
- What's stopping you?
- Where can you get that information?
- What are the 5 most important things in your life? What else do you want?
- What excites you and makes you feel alive?
- What makes you smile? How can you add more of that to your day? To your life?
- If you were to paint a picture of your life one year from now, what would it be?
- How have you changed from when you were 10 years old? 20? 30?
- If your life were represented by a color in this exact moment, what would it be? Why? What does this color mean to you?
- Imagine you were 95. What would you like to say about your life?
- Let's set a deadline. When do you want to accomplish this by?
- How will you know you have accomplished it?

2

Relationship Questions

Relationships are the best part of life. Every relationship takes time and effort from both people and requires a level of understanding about why another person does the things he or she does. It is important to know what a person is looking for and what he or she wants out of the relationship. Both parties need to be benefiting or else the relationship will not last.

Therefore, these are the questions that can be used to get to the bottom of what a person *really* wants in a relationship.

- What would you rate your current relationship on a scale of 1 to 10 (with 1 being terrible and 10 being excellent)?
- What do you like about your relationship?
- What do you want more of in your relationship?
- When you think of this relationship, how does it make you feel?

- What is something you've wanted to tell your partner but have resisted due to fear?
- What do you want?
- What are the 3 most important qualities that your partner must have?
- What are the 3 qualities that you cannot stand in a partner?
- Can you see yourself with him/her 20 years from now?
- What do you want more of?
- What is the first step to getting more of what you want?
- What does your intuition say?
- Who are you in the relationship?
- What have you learned from your past (or current) relationship(s)?
- What would your life be like if this person were to die tomorrow?
- What would you tell this person if you knew that today was his/her last day?
- Who do you have to be to attract this type of person?
- When do you want this by?
- Where do these types of people hang out? Where else?
- How would your best friend (or the person who knows and understands you best) describe you?
- Let's say a similar situation happens again. What would you do differently?
- Looking at the big picture, how important is this to you?

3

Fun Questions

Life was meant to be fun–it is a necessity in life. We work in order to have fun and enjoy time with ourselves and our families. Fun can range from relaxing on a couch and laughing at a sitcom on television to having an adventure at an amusement park with family.

This category was created to open doors to what a person wants for fun and how he or she can bring more fun into his or her life.

- What do you want more of in your life?
- What does fun mean to you? What else?
- If you had more fun in your life, how would that feel?
- When you are having fun, who do you see with you?
- On a scale of 1 to 10 (with 10 being the highest), what do you rate the level of fun in your life today? Where do you want it to be tomorrow? One week from now? One month from now?

Happiness

- How important is fun to you?
- When you were 10 years old, what was fun to you? What if you were to bring that feeling back into your life?
- What if we were to remove fun from your life? What would your life be like?
- If you had one day that was dedicated to having fun, what would you do?
- What is one thing you've always wanted to do but haven't due to fear?
- How can you bring more fun into your life?

4

Health Questions

Without health, we would not be alive. It is a topic that needs to be addressed for the completion of the 7 categories of personal development.

- What does it mean to you to be healthy?
- What would you rate your current level of health on a scale of 1 to 10 (with 10 being excellent)? What do you want it to be?
- What would you look like if your health was a 10? How would you feel?
- What would your day look like if your health was a 10?
- What do you want to improve?
- What is possible?
- What else?
- Who will support you?
- What are the other options?
- What is best for you?
- What are the consequences of not improving your health?

- When do you want to accomplish this by?
- Why do you want this?
- If your life depended on taking action, what would you do today? Tomorrow?
- How will you know when your health is a 10?

5

Career Questions

A person's career can bring a huge amount of happiness (or sadness) to his or her life. Therefore, one needs to get clear on what it is that will make them happy (which is the primary goal of humans worldwide), as a large part of one's life will be spent working at a career you either love or hate.

- If you could do anything and knew you couldn't fail, what would you do? Why?
- Who do you have to be (an adjective, or a real or fictional person) to get where you want to be?
- Who do you admire? What would he/she say to you right now?
- What is your greatest strength? How can you bring more of that to you current (or future) career?
- What are you passionate about? What things get you excited?

- Is money or job satisfaction more important to you?
- How do you believe that money and career are related? How does that apply to your life?
- What are you afraid of?
- Can you be more specific?
- What area do you need more clarity with?
- Who can you talk to in order to get more clarity on your decision?
- What would it feel like to be there (or have that career)?
- Let's set a deadline. When do you want this by?

6

Money Questions

Money. It keeps the world going around. Money gives people the opportunity to travel, fulfill wants and needs, and provide for a family. The lack of it causes much pain and hardship. To some it is important above all things, and to others it is toward the bottom of the ranking, below relationships, health, and career satisfaction.

This section will guide you with questions surrounding the field of money.

- If I was to give you 1 million dollars today, what would you do with it? How important is that to you? One year from now, how will you feel about the way your money was spent?
- What are the possibilities?
- What are your fears (around money)?
- What do you need to say no to in your life in order to make more money?
- What do you need?
- What do you want to make more money for?
- Who do you want to make more money for?

- What will more money bring you?
- What's stopping you from achieving your financial goals?
- What mindset do you need to have to accomplish this?
- Who are you? Create a metaphor (e.g., I am the glorious money tree who attracts money and gives others what they need).
- What does success mean to you?
- How will others perceive you if you reach your financial goals? Is that important to you?
- What will you need to do to achieve this?
- What are the consequences of not achieving your financial goals?
- What is the action plan?
- When will you have X amount of money by?

7

Physical Location Questions

To some, physical location matters above all else. Some dream of being on the beaches of Hawaii, whereas others dream of being in the mountains of Park City, Utah. If a person wants it bad enough, he or she will do whatever it takes to get there and then start a life. It happens every day. This section will help people get clear on this part of their life.

- What do you rate your level of happiness with your physical location (on a scale of 1 to 10, with 10 being the highest)?
- Where do you want to be?
- If you could live anywhere, no restrictions, where would it be?
- Imagine your ideal location. What is around you (e.g., mountains, beaches, farms)?
- What are the people like?
- Who else is there?
- What does your life look like on a daily basis?
- How important is it for you to get there?

Happiness

- What is stopping you from getting there?
- What are you afraid of?
- What excites you?
- How would you feel if you never achieved it?
- What do you need more of? What can you do to get it?
- When do you want to be there? How will it feel once you are there?

8

Master Questions for Elaboration and More Coaching Questions

These are the questions to get more information out of people. Best of all, the information gathered will come from a place of curiosity as opposed to a place of judgement, so the person will be more likely to respond favorably. These questions often lead to places you never knew existed. They will boost conversations and keep them going for hours.

- What do you mean by that?
- Let's take an outside perspective. What does your life look like now?
- What is important about that?
- What does that mean to you?
- What is your perspective? What is another perspective?
- How do you see it?
- What would that look like?
- How do you feel about that?
- Can you tell me more?
- What's stopping you?

Happiness

- What do you want from today's session?
- What is worse–failing or never trying?
- If you could offer a child one word of advice, what would it be?
- How can you bring more joy to your life?
- Are you living for yourself or for someone else?
- What other thoughts do you have about this?
- How else do you feel about this?
- Can you give me an example?
- What have you learned?
- So what's the advice here?
- Do you need a reminder? What can you use to remind yourself?
- One year from now, what will you think about today?
- Are you ready to make a commitment?
- Would you like me to hold you accountable?
- Where are you now (in the present moment)?
- What is the emotion here? Tell me about it.
- What's your body telling you? What are you noticing?

Afterword

Some say money makes the world go around, but I believe questions make the world go around because without questions there would be no money. It would be a world filled with assumptions and judgments without taking one's point-of-view into account. It would be a world filled with confusion and a lack of clarity.

My request for you (if you haven't already) is to go out and use these questions every day in your conversations. You will find more meaning in all of your relationships and get more clarity for your own and others' journeys with personal development. Use the questions to get clear on what it is you truly want.

Use these questions to coach yourself and others to strengthen relationships, improve health, and advance careers. I encourage you to look back on these questions and review your previous answers to monitor your personal growth and progress.

Section II. Be Happy NOW

Preface

This section contains proven-to-work strategies for washing away the darkness of your past, transforming your fears for the future into feelings of joy and excitement, and most importantly, steering you into a new life in the present moment. This is the land where you create your future, and wipe away your past. Stories from people I had the opportunity of coaching, as well as my countless struggles and incredible triumphs, will be sprinkled throughout to paint a vivid picture in order to inspire. It will bring you more out-of-the-box ideas of how you can easily access and live in the present moment.

You will understand how to completely shift your perspectives on how you feel about your life. Feelings of worry and fear will transform into feelings of tranquility and freedom while you're in the present moment. This will be a journey showing you how the past is like a beautiful old, soft, withered flower filled with wisdom from what you've been through. But your past shouldn't be something to hold on to for too long or replay over and over. Then we will transition into the future, fantasizing about your dreams and desires, while intertwining bits of the incomparable present moment throughout the section. You will understand the powerful strategies of living in the present moment and how to apply them faster than you can snap your fingers.

I have kept an effective algorithm in the back of my mind for years now: it's that each day 80% of your thoughts should be devoted to the present moment for boosting productivity, engaging in meaningful conversations, and simply enjoying your time on earth; and 10% should be given to learning from the past. Last, but not least, is to give the remaining 10% to the future for planning your day. This is the formula for happiness and peace of mind.

The beginning of my dark past

I spent much of my life living in the past and asking the question "Why me?" after my family and I were in a plane crash that killed my mother and almost killed me. I was in a coma for a month having to relearn all the basic functions for another three months, including how to walk, talk, and even hold a pen to scribble my name. It was difficult to let go of the past and move forward with my life, knowing that life will never be the same because I'd never see my mom again.

Having a permanent disability that made simple tasks, such as holding a pen, holding a fork, typing, and other fine motor tasks difficult to do was especially embarrassing as a young kid. The funny thing was that at first glance no one would ever expect me to have those disabilities. Therefore, in social situations I'd often be worried because I would wonder what others were thinking of me, such as "What's wrong with him?" and "Why does he write so sloppy and slow?"

Preface

I would be "having a conversation" with someone and at the same time I'd be thinking about things I wanted to do later that day. I was there, but not *there*. It's like you are given this present (the present moment), and you can either take it by staying in the present moment, or push it away (staying in the past and rejecting the future because of a monster called FOU (fear of the unknown)). I would worry about things that were probably *never* going to happen. I needed to get a grasp and understand myself so that I could focus on my strengths, instead of thinking about my imperfections. This would have allowed me to focus on the present moment and fully embrace my strengths because I was missing out on life, which only exists in the present moment.

I was stuck in a state of anxiety because I was living in my head too much, missing out on the beauty of life around me, and the world inside my body – the present moment.

Over the next five years, I began to do a lot of personal development work with the intention of "fixing" my imperfections. Throughout this time, I read several books including *How To Win Friends and Influence People* by Dale Carnegie, *7 Habits of Highly Effective People* by Steven Covey, and *The Power of Now* by Eckhart Tolle. These books opened my eyes and showed me the power of goal-setting and most importantly, embracing the present so that I can enjoy every moment and feel grateful for what is already there. *I am grateful for things from the beauty of being able to feel oxygen entering my mouth, flowing through my throat, and spreading through my lungs. I am grateful for my ability to feel emotions. I'm grateful for my ability to connect with other humans by exchanging words and feeling what the other person is really saying in the present moment.*

I'm not sure, but I imagine you want the ability to feel

Preface

less stressed and enjoy life more, or the ability to sink into the present moment. Maybe you are too focused on events that have already happened, such as a death, a break-up, or a stressful event at work. Maybe you are too busy planning things or multi-tasking. Maybe you feel like your mind is racing at a million miles per hour and you can't stop to say "Hello" to yourself because you left yourself miles down the road at the last rest stop. What if you were to slow down, feel the beauty of your breath inside your body, and embrace the present moment?

I have learned, seen, and felt how transformative the present moment is – similar to taking a sinking ship safely to shore. It gives me the space to have the most amazing conversations and connect at a level I have never experienced before. It has shown me how to accept the things I can't change (the past) place less worry and fear toward the unknown (the future) and most importantly, to enjoy the present moment, which is where life exists.

My request for you as you are reading this book, is to hone in on the present moment, have a clear mind, and remember that the past is over. It is the present moment that dictates your future. With that being said, let's take a breath, let's silence our cell phones, focus on the fact that you are alive, and feel grateful for this moment in which your life will never be the same.

Matt Morris, CPCC

Introduction

Take a minute to get fully present, free from distractions. Let's turn off our cell phones (or at least put them on silent and flip them over so that you can't see the screen), turn off our social media (especially Facebook, where we get bombarded with so much Newsfeed that we often forget what we were doing in the first place), and get fully present. Hone in to this very moment. I strongly encourage you to fully engage yourself when reading this book so that you can soak up every last word in hopes that you resonate with the stories you are about to read.

Let's begin with a story about a king of the medieval times who was told by the chief physician of his court that he will be paralyzed in exactly 10 years. After examining him thoroughly, the physician also advised him to beget a son who could not only move his dynasty forward, but could also take care of him once he became paralyzed because the physician was sure of his diagnosis. The king had a very angry temperament. Hearing these words, he ordered his men to kill the physician at once. He also ordered his men to search for his son, whom he had booted from the kingdom two years back because he insisted on marrying the daughter of the king's enemy.

The King's son was not found as he had fled to some distant land with the princess of the enemy's kingdom. Over the next 10 years of his life, the King kept marrying different women, who, to his surprise, gave him only girl children. He would kill all those little princesses because in that kingdom, it was a common belief that women were far weaker than men. The disappointed king spent those 10 years lamenting about his past mistake of kicking his son out of his kingdom as well as worrying about himself becoming paralyzed in the near future.

After a few more years, he had given up on trying to have a son. He would spend his mornings in depression with the thoughts of his past mistakes and his evenings with the worries of his dreadful future.

The King started losing control over the administration of his kingdom so much that in the 10th year of his mindlessness (as opposed to mindfulness), some tribal kings had already captured the peripheries of his kingdom. Finally, his own trusted men of the court started becoming treacherous; one of them gained control over others and threw this depressed king into jail. His 10th year had passed, then the 11th year passed and he still didn't have any symptoms of paralysis at all, ever. He spent the rest of his life in jail, lamenting and thinking about his past and future, which were ruined by his self-defeating thoughts. He also reminisced the decisions he made years ago and how they could have completely changed the road to his future.

Was the king foolish or wise? He could have searched again for his son, or he could have found another physician to correctly diagnose, or even prevent any paralysis over the 10-year period. He could have made his daughters so skilled that they would have become efficient queens of his

Introduction

kingdom, as well as take care of his ailment once it started bothering him. Most importantly, he could have enjoyed his 10 years in happiness, living in his present moments. Maybe he could have lived his life as a king in a lavish manner, doing the things that make him happy. However, he chose to be caught up in the thoughts and mistakes of his past and the worries for the future.

The situations of the contemporary people of the world are similar to that of the King. Every single person is given the ability to joyfully experience the present moment, however millions of people "choose" to lament over past mistakes or traumatic events. They often fear that tomorrow will swallow them up. We don't know if the world will end in five seconds, therefore, place your conscious mind in the present moment, and *choose* to live now.

Matt Morris, CPCC

Dr. Shah Faisal Ahmad

9

Pieces of Your Identity

Pieces of Your Identity

A person's identity is created by past moments, present experiences, as well as dreams for the future. The past plays a significant role in how a person chooses to live life because it has contributed to the formation of *who* a person has become. It is the catalyst to which beliefs are formed to design your future.

More often than not, it's difficult to let go of a traumatic past and it is a constant challenge to stop feeling anxious about the future. Perpetual happiness in life is closely tied to your ability to let go of your past and understand that those past events are over. Therefore, if traumatic past experiences are dwelled on for too long it can lead to depressing thoughts, including what you *could have* or *should have* done to the point where you feel stuck. The reality is that those are things you cannot change because that time has passed.

People have a very hard time releasing things because they think they'll crumble once these things are gone. This is why it's important to know that how you see yourself affects your decision on what to let go of. The thoughts you choose to keep in the cloud of thoughts bouncing in your mind will either negatively or positively influence your current state.

Jack, a 55-year old man was a highly successful businessman who was flying high in his private jet soaring from city to city. He had offices from Seattle to San Diego and all along the west coast of the United States. Just five years earlier, he lost his wife due to a car accident in which he was the driver. Every day of his life, he felt guilty and constantly blamed himself for her death. He crumbled, began to use drugs, and eventually lost his business.

Sleeping on the streets of San Francisco, he had hit rock bottom and felt he had nowhere to go. One day, feeling ashamed, he took a look at his life and what had happened to him and screamed, "ENOUGH!" He was determined to shift his perspective from feeling worthless to feeling fully capable and in control of his future. It started with focusing on the simple things he could immediately feel gratitude for – being alive, the sunshine, God, and living in one of the most beautiful cities (San Francisco). From that day forward, every morning and night he would stand up and speak aloud of at least three things he felt grateful for.

You can choose what you think about and your thoughts will change how you feel. Let's play for a few minutes. Take a second to think of a depressing thought and dwell on it for a minute. Maybe it was the time a loved one died, or you found out your lover didn't love you anymore, or the time you failed an exam.

Then take a few seconds to shift your body, change your posture, and take a deep breath. Spend the next minute thinking of an amazing experience you'd had in your life and smile about it. Maybe it was when you found an amazing job after searching for months, or when your child was born, or when you had a conversation with someone with whom you deeply connected.

How do you feel?

This is to point out that we have a *choice* in feeling the way we feel, simply by shifting our bodies and shifting our thoughts.

YOUR STORY

You have a story. Some of the parts to your story are relevant to the improvement of your life. It is what you create that gives you an idea of what has helped mold you into who you have become. Your story consists of triumphs and failures, which are opportunities to learn from so that you can flourish. These moments are what make life most rewarding because one day you can look back and feel bliss over what you have overcome or accomplished.

When I was a teenager, I had severe back problems due to a 45-degree curvature of my spine (scoliosis). That made it painful and difficult to walk or even stand up straight. There was not a clear explanation of why I had significant back problems for the previous three years. However, at the time I had two options. I could either have back surgery (as doctors recommended), hoping that it would go well; or I could devise my own plan to improve my back. In the meantime, doctors provided me with a hard plastic back brace that covered my whole torso to stabilize my back. During this time, my back muscles had significantly deteriorated because the brace was not allowing me to use my muscles. Therefore my scoliosis got worse as my muscles weakened. I felt hopeless and often had thoughts of suicide feeling I was less worthy than my peers.

I had to come up with a plan because I was not going to let this disability kill me. I was afraid to have back surgery, and frankly I didn't want to have a rod in my back for the rest of my life. I spoke with several health professionals from physical therapists and personal trainers to yoga masters asking them what they recommend I do. Naturally, the responses were to exercise and strengthen my muscles around my back to straighten my spine. In addition, it was equally important to be fully present when performing these exercises, to feel and listen to what my body was saying. After two weeks of doing exercises every day (squats, lunges, and sit-ups) and being fully present while performing them, I began to feel improvements. This was it - I had to regularly do these exercises for as long as I could. After doing these exercises consistently for only four months, I had improved significantly. Within six months I could walk pain-free, without a noticeable limp in my walk.

Your past can either build you up or bring you down. Many people who are stuck in the past cannot seem to get past the hurdle to feel good enough to let go and move forward. However, there are just as many people who are able to use what they have experienced as a way to learn and improve their current situation.

One of the first steps to overcome the past is to fully experience and genuinely feel the pain and hurt you've experienced. The worst thing is to ignore what you are feeling or "sweep it under the rug" for an extended period of time because the feelings will return, whether it be consciously or subconsciously. For example, if you are feeling sad or helpless, accept it and take the next moments to feel sad, instead of dodging your feelings or acting like you are happy.

It is important that your thoughts, words, and actions are aligned with everything you do because you are being honest with your mind, and body. People will appreciate that you are being honest with how you are feeling in the present moment.

Rick and his wife were headed to a Christmas Party that Rick did not feel like attending. He was tired after a long, stressful day at work. After a few minutes of his wife convincing him to go, he decided to do it and simply embrace how he was feeling. Therefore, at the party when someone asked him how he was, he would respond with how he was feeling - "tired"- and then he would briefly explain why. Some of the people would respond with silence or a "sorry to hear that", whereas others would try to relate to him and talk about how tired or stressed they themselves felt. After Rick embraced his tiredness for a good 30 minutes, he began to feel better, re-energized, and enjoyed himself at the Christmas party.

Your emotions in the present moment will shift. Sometimes you will feel anxious, tired, or frustrated because we are all human and everyone experiences these blasts of emotion. Therefore, there is no reason to feel ashamed or embarrassed or any less than perfect if you do not always have a smile on your face, appearing to be happy. I see perfection as simply being your authentic self, having your thoughts, words, and actions aligned so that you are being completely honest with yourself, respecting how you are feeling as an individual.

Recognizing the emotion you are feeling only takes a few seconds and once you understand how you are feeling, you'll feel an underlying sense of bliss. Once you choose to embrace the emotions you feel and take the time to experience them, they will naturally flow in and out of your body and mind. It's important to feel the way you feel as opposed to avoiding certain emotions. Sometimes it's challenging to name the emotion you are feeling. Therefore, we will look at ways to easily identify the emotions in order to be acutely aware of how you are feeling.

LET the past be your guide

Some people see the world as black and white, or right and wrong with very little gray, believing that there is only one way to see things. However, every situation can be colorful and rainbowesque in that there are a number of ways to look at a situation. Ask 10 people the same open-ended question and you will get 10 different answers consisting of a wide range of perspectives, opinions, and beliefs. It is a refreshing feeling to understand that it is never too late to live a good life in the present moment, by simply shifting your current perspective of a situation.

If you are struggling with something, exploring your past and assessing how you have gotten to this point in time can help bring you closer to the stage of letting go. Ask your parents, other relatives, or friends to tell you what they know about your situation in order to gain new perspectives and understand the past.

YOU AND YOUR Identity

It is necessary to relate your identity to your willingness to learn from your past mistakes and failures. You are the only one who has the power to release the chains holding you back. Many people spend their lives beating themselves up over past mistakes (e.g. drugs, alcohol, emotional abuse, physical abuse) instead of taking the time to stop and fully understand what the lesson is from the past mistake(s), which will allow them to prepare for a similar situation in case it happened again. It is impossible to change the past, but it is important to keep in mind that your current identity is who you are today, in this moment.

Jane had a tendency to fill her days up by saying "Yes" too often. She said "Yes" to far more things than she said "No" to. Therefore, people perceived her as flaky and not true to her word. She saw herself as a people pleaser who wanted to make everyone happy. In spite of this, she felt like a failure because she had not spent enough time striving for her personal goal of starting her own business, and several relationships suffered because she wasn't able to nurture them due to the fact that she said "Yes" too often.

This had to come to an end. She committed to getting realigned with her priorities by asking herself "What is truly important to me? Why it is important?" She created a schedule to manage both her social time and her business time (via Google Calendars on her mobile devices). She fully committed to saying "No" with a simple explanation of why she couldn't say "Yes".

Keep in mind that your Past-self does not exist anymore. Yesterday is gone. All of those traumatic or depressing memories of the past are over, and it is time to say goodbye. Your Present-self should realize that you should not allow the unchangeable to govern your life and lead you to believe that you are less than your Future-self. Take time to explore your past and then commit to letting go of it. Your past is like a rock you're tossing into the sea.

Take time to absorb each and every area of your life. The road to healing from the past is not always an easy or a short one, but it is a necessary one in order to live in the present moment. The way you view yourself and your life should not be dependent on what has transpired, but rather the person you choose to be this second.

THE CONSTANT TRANSFORMATION

The skill to live in the present moment is not an overnight transformation. It is a daily process and shift in awareness that will eventually form into a powerful habit. It takes effort to be aware of your thoughts and notice when your thoughts drift into the past or the future when you are having a conversation with others. You may notice yourself escaping the present with thoughts of how you forgot to take out the trash on Tuesday and how it will pile up until next week, or how you are expecting your boss to respond once you tell him that you still haven't completed that project. They are completely irrelevant in this moment.

Happiness

Courtney had trouble listening and retaining what others were saying. She would often hear them, but wouldn't fully understand them. She had a tendency to be easily distracted by other things in the environment, other than the person with whom she was talking. People perceived her as aloof and forgetful. She claimed she had Attention Deficit Disorder, even though she had never been diagnosed.

Courtney made it a goal of hers to be more present in conversations because that was the person she wanted to be. Every time she had a conversation with someone, she would create an imaginary bubble surrounding her and the other person she was talking with as if they were the only people who existed on the planet. It was not easy but repetition turned it into a beautiful habit.

PUTTING the Pieces Together

Perhaps you are wondering how you can fully live in the present without being absorbed by regrets and worries. The fact is that everyone has regrets and worries, but the key difference between people is how each person responds to those feelings. Maybe you think it is not possible to be de-stressed about the past or anxiety-free about the future and you feel hopeless. Understand that the best is yet to come as you discover more about what is possible in the present moment.

You may be aware of your personality strengths and weaknesses, but the true power comes by focusing on the present moment, where you can become fully aware of the possibilities of which you are capable.

Stop for a moment and listen to what's around you. Listen to what is going on in your body. How is your posture? How is your breathing? Can you feel your heart beating inside your chest? How are you feeling? Name the emotions, and take the time to *really* feel them. If you feel happy, really *feel* happy; if you feel angry, really *feel* angry;

if you feel excited, really *feel* excited. Locate where you feel it in your body and touch it. Does fear cause an aching in your chest? Does excitement make you feel tingly all over your body? Listen to your body, and be aware of it so that you can begin to name your emotions as you feel them.

I went on a personal retreat to the magnificent Joshua Tree National Park. There, I wanted to get a better grasp on my emotions to recognize how I was feeling, what thoughts triggered specific emotions, and what I felt in my body when the emotion was triggered. In order to do this, I wanted a silent place where I could connect with nature – a place of solitude. A place where I could completely be in touch with my emotions in order to completely feel how I was feeling. For five days I documented all my thoughts, emotions, and how it felt in my body at specific times of the day. I discovered emotions that I had denied for many years, including jealousy, anger, and sadness. I had to separate myself from my Past-self and understand that it was okay to feel negative emotions and let them go.

Your goal may be to completely exist in the present so that you can find what you're looking for – possibly happiness or maybe a better and more meaningful existence. Remember your identity is who you are today, right now, not who you were years ago or who you want to be years from now.

Be present. Remember that you are here now, so experience it. In this section, you will be given inquiries or steps to take so that you can easily access the present and be able to remain in it for a considerable amount of time.

Take a moment to completely understand that yesterday is over, last year is over, the last minute is over - the past is the past and cannot change. The present is waiting for you to jump in and absorb. Relax, take a few deep breaths, and clear your mind. Experience what it is like to live life in the present moment.

For the next 7 days, remind yourself to be present. Start today by taking everything a little slower so that you can fully embrace each activity. When you sit, take notice of the surface you've chosen to sit on. Is it soft, squishy, rough, or hard? As you eat, taste the foods as if you are tasting them for the first time. Allow your curiosity to run free.

When your thoughts shift to the past (and they will), shift your focus on how you're breathing and how you're feeling in the moment. A few reminder strategies include putting sticky notes around your room, changing your screen saver to "BE IN THE PRESENT MOMENT", or buying a bracelet to use as a reminder so that each time you glance at it, you can shift yourself back into the present moment.

10

Letting Go Of Your Past

Letting Go Of Your Past

Relationships are one of the most rewarding parts of life. The ability to connect with another person and feel like someone truly understands you is an incredible feeling. On the other hand, relationships can complicate a person's story and make it a constant struggle to let go of things. It's ironic to think that what can bring a person so much joy can also be the same thing that makes a person's blood boil.

Johnny had begun a new relationship with Stephanie. After four months of going out, he noticed aspects of his work and social life diminishing because he was consumed with thoughts of his new lover. These thoughts often consisted of fear and jealousy, and he would notice himself getting mad for unexplainable "demons in his mind". He feared that when he wasn't with Stephanie that she was seeing other men, and giving them attention that he felt only he deserved. He had no valid reason to accuse her of cheating on him. However, his ex-girlfriend had left him broken hearted after he caught her cheating on him. He was carrying this incident into his new relationship.

After a few angry outbursts and senseless accusations, he realized he needed to do something about his irrational jealousy. He decided that whenever he began to feel jealous, he would take a moment to remind himself that his past relationships had absolutely nothing to do with his current one, and to focus on the present moment. He'd concentrate on the environment he was in – whether it be the supermarket, his office, or his own bedroom – then he would observe his surroundings and take it all in with a perspective of "fascination", similar to when a child sees something incredible for the first time. Then, he'd focus on the single task he was performing – whether it be finding a delicious looking tomato in the grocery store, concentrating on his assignment at work, or the suspenseful novel he was reading in his bedroom – instead of letting his mind wander into feelings of fear and jealousy.

Family, friends, and old or recent lovers can make life quite colorful, both in pleasurable and distasteful ways. Since the relationships in your life have such a strong impact on how you feel, detaching yourself from past issues, severing unhealthy relationships, and letting go of the small stuff are clear musts. You do not deserve to be chained to people or things that diminish your joy and peace in the present.

Those closest to you can be the most dangerous. No one is saying that your mother, father, or siblings have plans to hurt you, but serious problems or issues in the immediate family can directly impact your decisions and how you feel about them. It's normal for families to undergo stressful emotional and mentally exhausting problems, but these don't have to last as long as most people allow them to. Issues that don't get resolved fairly quickly can become more complex problems that create a cage around a person's heart.

FAMILY

Forgive them and let go of the pain

You have to realize that what often cages you is under your own control, especially if it stems from the past. Bitterness or grudges toward family members do not affect the recipient as much as they affect the one harboring them. Often times, when people experience these feelings toward relationships, it feels like a mind-blockage that is restricting creativity and freedom. Creativity soars when your mind is clear in the present moment, allowing you to reach a level of brilliance that's hard to find.

It's time to let go of the pain you've been bottling up inside from a burnt relationship – for example, one tied to your mother or an ex-lover, or a co-worker. Things may have not turned out the way you intended but that is in the past – it's over so you must move forward with your life, or else this lingering pain will remain. The sooner you confront and resolve the issue, no matter how painful you imagine it being, the sooner you will feel better about your past, present, and future.

Jennifer was disappointed and hurt because her dad missed her wedding ceremony. She knew her dad was not the most reliable person, as he'd often not stuck to his word. However, she was completely devastated that her dad was not at her wedding. She let this linger in her mind, and never confronted or forgave her dad for this upset. She was waiting for an apology. However, it was eating her alive.

Years had gone by and she had built up anger toward her dad whenever his name was mentioned or the thought of him entered her mind. They grew more distant. She would communicate with him only a few times each year, and each time she thought he would give an apology. This issue needed to get resolved to bring her peace of mind. She finally sat down with him, confronted him about the issue (that he had no idea was still bothering her) and after many tears from both her and her father, she chose to forgive him for missing her wedding. A new chapter in her life had reluctantly, yet blissfully, opened.

If a family member has admitted their mistakes and is now making an effort to come back to you with renewed commitment and love, be fast to forgive. They are boldly and courageously apologizing for what has happened in the past, and looking for a fresh start. Give yourself and your family member the pleasure of moving from the past and being in the present moment. Of course, it is impossible to completely wipe away the past, but it is possible to give people another chance.

Since it is the present moment that defines people, not the past, you have the option of letting go of the past by opening your hands, eyes, and heart to the present and accepting this person back into your life, regardless of their imperfections. Empty yourself of the guilt and anger you felt towards this relationship, allowing the feelings of love, joy, and acceptance to flood into your heart and soul.

You can't choose the family you are born into, but you can choose who you become – despite what you've experienced or how you may have been mistreated by those whom you love. Forgiveness is one of the most powerful gifts we can give, and even though letting go of the negative feelings may seem inconceivable at the moment, don't close your heart to it.

Forgiveness is one of the keys to living in the present moment. When you can forgive others and forgive yourself, you can begin to clear your mind of the guilt and shame that clouds your mind. Go ahead and do yourself a favor by extending love to your family despite their shortcomings and mistakes.

ACCEPT responsibility for your actions

When bad things happen, it is easy to place the blame on anyone or anything besides ourselves because it feels better, temporarily. Without accepting responsibility for our actions, it is easy to believe that every single person and every single thing in the world is out to get us. If you did something, you did it – it is a fact. Do not lie, or blame someone else for your actions. You may have been influenced by others to do what you did, but ultimately it was your choice, not anyone else's. Keep in mind that you are not less of a person because everyone makes mistakes no matter how impeccable you think someone may be.

The reason this is important is because by admitting your actions, you clear up your mind so that you can enjoy the present moment. It is challenging to remember the lie that you created, so begin with the truth because it will set you free. Initially, you first may feel guilty, embarrassed, or uncomfortable when admitting your mistake, and afterwards your mind forgives, letting the mistake go. Whereas if you decide to lie about it, then your thoughts, words, and actions are not aligned, and this mistake will be harder to permanently let go.

If taking responsibility for your mistakes is new to you, then it will feel uncomfortable. However, after doing it a few times it won't be nearly as uncomfortable, and will actually feel rewarding. People will appreciate the fact that you are being honest with yourself and being a human, who will inevitably make mistakes.

THE BUCKETS

Once you are in the habit of accepting responsibility for your actions – you can move from the past. One way to move beyond the past is to "wash it away" in a bucket of the past. I suggest putting two buckets in your bedroom – one being for good memories (the reminisce bucket) and one being for past, shameful memories (the trash bucket) that you've been holding on to.

The reminisce bucket is a tool you can use to receive an immediate feeling of joy, nostalgia, and gratitude. It is an amazing way of reminiscing about the past that will bring a smile and immediate sense of joy to your life. So go ahead and jot down five or ten memories on small pieces of paper that you want to keep, and place them in your reminisce bucket.

I suggest adding memories or gratitudes to this bucket regularly (daily, weekly) so that you make a habit of utilizing the buckets. This way you will remember to look into the reminisce bucket when you are having a rough day or are having trouble seeing the good side of life.

Once the buckets are in place, go ahead and write the memories on little pieces of paper. Next, I toss the shameful pieces of paper in the "trash" bucket. Then, either kiss them goodbye or burn them - get rid of them! This is a supernatural experience, a way of physically and spiritually "letting go".

FRIENDS

Friendship is a gift. It should be based on love and respect. If it feels like a burden where you have to constantly worry whether you're still friends due to a brief misunderstanding, then it is best to get the issue resolved as quickly as possible otherwise it will keep you in a state of worry and anxiety.

Tracy wanted to be liked by everyone. She wanted to be everything to everyone, even if it meant putting others ahead of her. Three words to describe her would be sweet, nice, and caring. When she felt that someone did not like her or had a problem with her, she would feel anxious and her personality shifted from friendly and confident, to absent-minded and aloof.

Tracy didn't want to be perceived this way and the only way to overcome it was to go directly to the person she felt angst towards and ask them outright if she had done something to upset them or hurt their relationship. Most of the time the other person had no idea that she was feeling this way toward them, and other times they would express what was bothering them. After discussing it, she could choose to either keep the friendship or let it go based on the amount of value she received and the value she could bring to the relationship. Either way, the fact that she went directly to the person, as opposed to talking to other people or making assumptions in her head, brought her a sense of relief as it put out the fiery feeling of worry.

Friendships should allow easy access to being in the present moment. If you have to worry about whether or not someone is your friend, this immediately puts you into a state of anxiety and fear. Friendships should feel natural so that you feel comfortable *being yourself.*

A great friend will be there for you no matter what you're going through, no matter how strong the winds of adversity have become. A great friend will encourage and be excited for your life and your personal growth. They will accept you for who you are and not try to change your personality. You will feel comfortable around them, and at the same time they will be the first to give you constructive feedback or play devil's advocate, out of love, to make sure you are making the best decision for yourself.

Take a second to think about your best friendship.

- Does your friend help you see yourself more clearly, or is the glass becoming foggier?
- How do your friends' words and actions affect you?

- How do you feel when you are around this person?
- Do you like yourself more or less when you are around this person?

THE PEOPLE you keep in your life have the greatest impact. They will influence the way you live, and how you think about yourself and the world around you. Therefore, it is important for you to create bonds and friendships with people who add value (which could be love, care, and respect) to your life. Of course this is not a one-sided coin, as you must add value to your friends' lives in order to maintain the relationship.

ROMANTIC RELATIONSHIPS

Romantic relationships have the power to affect all areas of life, including health, finances, and overall happiness. They have a way of changing people - sometimes for the better, and sometimes for the worse. They can make people do things they would have never dreamt of doing before they fell in love. It is no surprise that people are more concerned about their love life than with any other area of their lives, so be vigilant with whom you fall in love with because he or she has the power to lift you up or completely crush your spirit.

Amanda had been married for seven years. The first five years were mostly happy, and the last two were a struggle, mostly because she felt restricted by her husband from pursuing the career she desired. She desperately wanted to go back to school to practice nursing. Financially they were okay, and her husband had a 10-year old boy from a previous marriage. He wanted her to remain a housewife and take care of their son.

The desire to become a nurse had been floating around in her mind for the past two years. She loved her husband and her son, but she refused to deny what her heart desired. After several arguments, her husband gave her an ultimatum: she could either remain a housewife and take care of their child until he was 18, or she could leave the family and pursue a career in nursing.

Even though Amanda wanted both, she felt pressured and didn't want to bring it up ever again because she feared losing her marriage. However, she knew that if she didn't pursue a career as a nurse, she'd live life with regret of not listening to her heart – always wondering, "How would my life have been if I pursued a career as a nurse?" Months later, she sat down with him to talk about how important it was for her to become a nurse and she went for it. Despite the ultimatum from her husband, they came to an agreement and she is currently in nursing school and still happily married.

Let's take a few minutes look at your romantic relationship.

- Do you like how you feel when you are around this person?
- Does your mind fill with regrets, and anxiety about what the person will say next? Or does this person make you feel comfortable with being completely in the present moment, allowing you to be yourself?
- Notice who you become when you are with your romantic partner. From an outside perspective, are you the person you want to be?

GAME TIME!

If you have a romantic partner, ask him or her if she will play a game with you. This is called the "Yes, I love you" game. Grab your partner by both hands and face each other. Stare deep into each others' eyes. Say, "I love you." Then, have your partner say, "I love you." Repeat this back and forth ten times. Close your eyes and feel the energy through your hands.

Next, as you're holding your partners' hands, look deep into each others' eyes. Now say "I'm in love with you." Have your partner say, "I'm in love with you." Repeat this 10 times. Close your eyes once again and feel the energy through your hands. Reflect on how it feels to say, "I'm in love with you," versus "I love you."

Do you feel like "I am in love with you," is more in the present moment than "I love you"?

Have fun with this!

CAREER OR WORK-RELATED Relationships

Your relationship with employers or co-workers affects your life and state of mind because they are either directly or indirectly connected to your quality of life (QoL). Thoughts of how you were treated by your past co-workers can either negatively or positively affect your psyche. Allow these past experiences to be lessons, and then let them go so that you can focus on what is here now, and where you are headed. It is sometimes challenging to let go especially because a portion of your heart and energy was given to each company you've worked for. But, it is the past so take the good experiences and lessons, and let it go.

In many companies, employees miss out on life because they get so consumed with making money. Don't pigeon-hole yourself in your own career and forget that you miss out on a more balanced life, in which you can be present and fully experience each moment.

Michael was a life insurance salesman who was making a six-figure income. He was determined to be the highest income earner in the sales division of the company. This came from a fear of being unhappy and poor, similar to how his life was when he was growing up in his parents' household. He thought that by constantly winning and earning so much money, that he would be happy. However, he was not enjoying the process of getting there. He was too busy and too tired to participate in all the other joys of life that were outside of work – reading books, staying physically active, and all the little things that made him feel good inside.

After confirming that this competitive nature was taking a toll on his happiness, he took a step back and asked himself what was truly important in life, and where did he want to be one year from then. He discovered that he wanted more quality friendships, more time with his family traveling to places he'd always wanted to see, and to pursue his childhood dream of becoming a martial arts instructor.

It is important to set financial goals to create the life you desire. However, it is one thing to be consumed by your future financial goals, and another thing to be making progress and enjoying the process with a more balanced life by doing what brings you joy.

The next part will discuss the importance of letting go and the power of forgiveness, as well as the secret components that are necessary to forgive yourself and others. Once again, no matter what type of relationship you're hung up on, don't let it consume you because the past is over and there is no going back.

- Are there people or things in your life that are bringing you down - taking away from your joy and happiness?
- What or who are they?
- What do they add to your life?
- What do they take away from your life and your ability to be present?
- How can you either change your perspective or cut them from your life?

11

A New Perspective

It is common to become overly attached to a situation from the past. This can lead to feelings of loneliness, depression, and helplessness, which can be followed by addictions. Some of these addictions include sex, drugs, alcohol, extreme expenditures, watching too much TV, as well as over-eating – all of which are destructive, especially if you let the habits get out of control.

The eyes are considered to be the windows to the soul. The lenses you use to view the world, your circumstances, and yourself *can* be changed. It's not really possible to completely *forget* about the past, but if you are able to develop a new way of looking at it, you will feel like a fresh wave just washed your soul.

Drugs can change the way you think about things, yet so can your mind by generating perspective shifts. One of the easiest and most powerful ways to remove a burden that has been hurting you for a long time is to use a perspective shift. Imagine how your life would be different if you took the perspective of "everything happens for a reason"? There is a reason you met that man in the coffee shop today that recommended you try a new type of latte, as opposed to your typical everyday morning latte. There is a reason the stoplight turned red even though you're late for work. There is a reason that you were mugged after walking home from a nice dinner with your sister. There is a reason you survived a plane crash. There is a reason your mom and dad died before you turned 30.

Each of these circumstances happened to me, and each of them were out of my control. I believe that since "everything happens for a reason", these circumstances occurred so that I could bring hope and inspiration to others' lives.

Do I like these situations? Of course not! Do I wish they hadn't turned out like that? Yes. Do I accept that as reality? Yes. Do I think those events happened for a reason? Yes. Even though many situations are out of our control, and feel beyond horrific, we still have the power to choose our perspective. What if you chose to believe that every terrible situation you experienced happened for a reason?

In Section II, I share several stories from my former coaching clients and students. I feel it's appropriate to share my own story with you here and now.

I was in a plane crash that killed my mother and left me in a coma for a month at the age of 10. I had to relearn all the basic functions including: reading, writing, walking, talking, etc. What was the reason for this disaster? My perspective is that I survived the plane crash because it is my mission to inspire and give hope to people all over the world who perhaps suffered a traumatic event themselves.

Take the time to ask yourself:

- What valuable information can I take from a past traumatic event that I've been holding on to?

- How can I look at this situation differently to use this to help myself, and others?

ADMIRATION PERSPECTIVE

If you can't think of another way to look at your situation, take a second to think of someone you truly admire. Put yourself in his or her shoes, and ask yourself "How would (the person you admire) look at this situation?"

You may not be able to change your circumstances, but you can change the way you see things. If you can find a way to look at this experience as an opportunity to grow, learn from, and make it your mission to help others, it will not only increase your present strength, but it will make the past seem less significant.

After you have a new perspective on your situation, take the life lessons from the situation you're facing and think of ways you can apply them to your life to add value to yourself and others' lives.

DUMP your junk

Break-ups, separations, and divorces are never easy. Even though there are several reason you ended the relationship, there will still be things you miss about the person. Maybe it was the sweet love letters you two wrote your ex at the beginning of your relationship. Maybe it was the passionate love making. Maybe it was how every morning your partner would make you breakfast and coffee. Whatever it is, there was a reason that the relationship ended, and it is time to let it go.

Cindy was suffering because she had gotten dumped by her boyfriend of 3 years, and "replaced" by a younger woman. She thought to herself "If only I were prettier, or smarter, or maybe I was too needy." Then she wanted to do whatever she could to get back with him. She constantly called and texted him. She would unexpectedly show up at his front door, hoping he would fall madly back in love with her. She wrote him a love letter, and texted him fun pictures from past times they shared together. Nothing worked, and she couldn't get him off her mind. Months went by and I introduced her to a powerful way of letting go of the past, called the "dump your junk" session.

If you have something that is still eating you away inside, perhaps a break-up, loss of a job, or a traumatic event from the past, you can use this method to "dump your junk".

Here is how it works:

Take a minute to close your eyes and visualize what happened during the event. Really feel the emotions. Feel how it feels to be in that place. How does it look? Is it colorful? Are the images moving? After you've have a strong grasp on how it feels to be in that place (almost to the point where you can't take it anymore), draw an imaginary box around it, and then with your hands squash the box so that it is tiny. While holding the imaginary box (with your memory in it), shout out "I'm done with you!" and take your hands and throw it in the dumpster to never be seen again.

Feel a sense of relief because that moment is gone from your life. It will not come back. And if it does, remind it of its place (the dumpster) and throw it back in there.

CHALLENGE your beliefs and assumptions

It is important to challenge the beliefs and assumptions that anyone who doubted you placed in your mind. Go out and test them in the real world and notice that you are fully capable of getting the results you want, whether it is getting a job you desire, or getting a romantic partner of your choice. Of course, much in life is a numbers game, so the more you do something (especially when you fail because it has a stronger emotional impact), the better you will get. It's similar to exercising a muscle in the gym – the more you exercise it, the stronger it'll get. So remember to keep on failing (and learning) because it will make you stronger the next time around.

Once you begin to look at your past differently, new doors will open, allowing you to get closer to letting go of the things that cause you pain. Anger, worry, and fear only blur your assessment of things, so it's better to take a look at the past more carefully and with an open mind. Think of a painful situation from the past and ask yourself:

- What is important about this event?
- How is it serving me?
- What have I learned about myself?
- What do I want now?

The answers to these questions will only come to those who earnestly and calmly seek them. Negative emotions and resentment-filled lenses will only cause you to suffer and remain stagnant.

MEDITATION

When you meditate, you empty yourself of all the toxins that are unhelpful to the development of inner peace. Meditation isn't limited to precise stretches, body positions, proper breathing, or a completely peaceful environment. Meditation can be done inside your room, in a quiet area. It is a way of accessing the present moment, letting thoughts flow in and out of your mind, like you are filling your mind up with water and then releasing it back into the universe. Experts say that it takes at least 12 minutes of meditation for it to have lasting positive benefits, including strengthening attention and working memory.

Take a few moments for the next exercise. Close your eyes to prevent your mind from external distractions. Think about the life you've been given – the ability to breathe, move, communicate, make decisions etc. – and feel a sense of gratitude for it. Let the past flow out of your system as you take deep breaths and let your mind wander into places where you've prohibited it to explore. Meditation gurus suggest having a mantra when you meditate. The most common one is repeating "ohm" in your mind as you begin to clear your head, relax, and de-stress. "Be" in a state of meditation for at least 12 minutes.

MEDITATION GIVES you clarity of mind

Meditation is one of the best ways to de-stress. As you meditate and allow your tensions to be released from your system, you'll be able to think more clearly. Meditation increases self-awareness and allows people to clear the mind and discover new things about themselves. For example, you may use it to realize why certain feelings came up during a particular event, why you approached a problem the way you did, what made you say what you said, and even get clear on what you want for each day.

"Where are you?" my friend Kyle asked as I picked up my fork and knife to cut into the delicious piece of steak in front of me.

"I don't know. I don't know if I made the right decision," I stuttered.

"What do you mean? You're not talking about Jenna again, are

you? Come on man. I know it was a tough breakup but you made the right decision."

"I keep going back and forth with it, and I just don't know. Maybe I should call her and apologize for breaking up with her. I feel down about it."

As Kyle and I were walking back to our cars it hit me. My intuition swept across me and whispered, "meditate about it", as I felt tingles run throughout my body. It had been months since I had meditated because I'd gotten so caught up in starting a new business. I had forgotten the powerful effects that meditation can give, especially when I needed clarity for complicated decisions, such as this one.

The next morning I spent in complete silence, meditating for 60 minutes and then writing down my thoughts and feelings. I also spent an hour in the evening to get clarity on my decision that the break-up was the best decision for me. Despite the love I felt, I came to the conclusion that I did not like the person I became when I was around her. I did not feel like my authentic self and from that point I knew I had made a good decision. The pressure I felt to go back into the relationship had completely dissipated.

You can solve many of your own problems if you're in the right state of mind. When you're not stressed, your mind will be more clear and creative. You'll have time to process everything and encourage yourself to naturally take the next step toward letting go of the past.

Know what's in your mind and heart so that you'll also know what you should do after your meditation time. Carl Jung, the founder of analytical psychology once said, "Your vision will become clear only when you can look into your own heart. Who looks outside, dreams; who looks inside, awakes."

As for me, I like to journal for five to ten minutes about my thoughts after I meditate and explore the meaning behind them. Other people like to engage in physical activity, such as running or biking. Whereas other people feel complete after the meditation is over and move forward with their day. Figure out what works best for you and you may find this to be a revolutionary experience for letting go of your past.

TAKE care of your body

As yoga experts claim, the condition of the body affects the condition of the mind and vice-versa. Take care of yourself by balancing your time. Don't immerse yourself in your work, school, or spend too much time doing one thing. Your body follows your mind. The way you feel about yourself shows by the way you carry yourself. If it is challenging to change your thoughts because you can't get something off your mind, such as a recent argument with your child or how you forgot to tell your partner that you loved him when he hung up the phone. Try shifting your body. First take a deep breath, put your shoulders back, stand up straight, and fully extend your arms as if you had just won a race. Hold it there for at least two minutes. Feel the power of your body working to change your mind. It has been proven that by extending your arms up in the air and holding it for two minutes, increases your drive and motivation. Here is a link to an amazing short Ted Talk video explaining the power of body language: https://www.**ted**.com/speakers/amy_cuddy

TEARS OF HEALING

Crying has a way of easing tension and releasing negative energy and emotions from your body. Biologically speaking, crying also releases toxins from the body. When people cry they feel much better because they are being true to their feelings. Of course, since most societies have not accepted crying in public, take the time to step into a private place and shed your tears as you feel necessary. Feel the sense of relief as you are releasing the tears of pain, hurt, anger, frustration, or whatever it may be. Give your tears permission to fall so that your pain can flow out of your body.

Telling yourself to not cry is cruel because you're not designed to just forget your pain by sheer willpower. Cry it out and shout if necessary, even if you only do it once. Sometimes, crying once is enough to help you move many steps closer to emotional and mental healing. It is a way of living naturally and reacting to your emotions, not running away from them.

When I found out that my dad had died, I was devastated, and full of anger because he wasn't supposed to die at the young age of 59. I felt like a huge chunk of my heart was ripped out. There was so much more that I wanted to ask him and experiences I wanted to share with him. However, at that moment I was angry, and I had to hold it in because I was in a public place, and I felt miserable. Once I stepped inside my home, I couldn't help myself from breaking down and crying as I fell to my knees screaming "Why?!" This lasted a few minutes, and then it repeated sporadically throughout the next few days. I felt temporarily better after crying and shouting, as opposed to holding it all in.

Crying your frustrations and pain away has also proven to be an effective way to move away from a painful past. Fully replay this experience in your mind to keep moving forward, get it out of your system, and put this past behind you by shedding tears of sorrow.

THE POWER of failure

Failure is the greatest teacher of all. Although it can feel embarrassing, depending on how serious you choose to take the mishap, it can also be a chief opportunity to understand what NOT to do, potentially saving you years of hardship. The incredible thing about failure is that it gives you a yellow light to change, in which you have a choice to improve a situation that isn't working. It is easy to put a ton of time and energy into something, only to find out that what you were working on was not meant to be.

Physical fitness, self-improvement, and psychology have always been passions of mine. I chose to pursue a career in physical therapy, which required mostly science courses to earn a Doctorate of Physical Therapy (which is required to practice physical therapy nowadays). However, science courses were classes I'd always struggled with, and consequently I knew it wasn't going to be easy.

I listened to my heart and chose to pursue a career as a Physical Therapist – which required years of science courses. Even though my heart told me that it was my mission to help people the way physical therapists had helped me over months of rehab, my mind was resisting because I knew how tough science courses were for me. I still went for it because I knew I'd regret it if I didn't at least try.

With hours and hours of studying science material, I got through the first year of physical therapy school. The second year I found myself struggling more because the science courses were more challenging for me, and on top of that I had to work twice as hard due to my disability with my right hand. Long story short, I ended up failing school. It wasn't meant to be, as my heart and mind were not aligned.

At first, I did not want to accept the failure. For months, I sent letters to the Dean explaining my circumstances and kept requesting to be re-admitted into the program. The Dean did not accept my request.

After feeling down and depressed for months, I decided to call an old friend to reconnect during lunch.

As I sat down he smiled and said, "I just got back from a meeting with my life coach." He sighed in relief.

With a confused look plastered on my face, I replied, "What is a life coach?"

"Oh it's great man. My coach helps me get back on track with my life purpose, and helps me achieve my goals by holding me accountable."

I thought to myself, "That is exactly what I need because I had no idea what I wanted to do with my life. I didn't understand why I was on this earth. I needed help."

The next day I called up a life coach and was blown away. As he was asking me questions to help me discover my life purpose, I was thinking to myself in complete ecstasy, "This is it! I want to do EXACTLY what he is doing. I want to ask powerful questions to help others discover things about themselves. I knew I loved helping people solve problems. I have always been into reading self-help books to discover ways to help myself and other people."

During the coaching session, we discussed my new discovery and he gave me the information for the school to attend and earn a Certificate to be a Certified Professional Coactive Coach (CPCC).

Everyday I am grateful for my decision to become a Life Coach. Failing physical therapy school taught me the power of failure, and showed me that, as the saying goes, when one door closes another one opens.

Failure can mold us into who we want to become, although it does not define who we are. Most people stop after they fail once, even though this is where the biggest opportunity for growth exists. That is, if you choose to take action by taking a keen look at the failure to see how you can improve yourself for next time, and then try again. It is the people who do keep on pushing and learning from their mistakes who are the most resilient, and given the most opportunities in life.

You should never consider yourself a failure, and you don't have to. We just have to look at failing as our willingness to try something that simply didn't work, and most importantly understand that the gift of failure is an opportunity to learn what *not* to do and change to what you can to improve the situation for next time.

If you want to live a life without failure, playing it safe all the time, you are missing out on life because your experiences will be limited. Therefore, embrace the fact that these are your experiences and they will continue to help mold you into a stronger and more persevering person.

I understand that it is easy to get stuck in the past and feel depressed about the failure. I understand that it is easy to keep your eye on the prize and miss out on enjoying the process of getting to the prize. However, it is important to not obsess about a future dream because then you will miss out on the little joys of each moment, and your future dream may seem so far away that you give up. If you take it day-by-day, making the most out of each day, eventually the dream will manifest itself and be part of your reality.

One of the most monumental mistakes with failure is admitting that you're wrong. Once you can accept the failure, you can move on from it and change. Again, it is what you do with the mistake that matters. Discovering the hidden gems, or the lessons from our failures is not always easy. This process becomes more challenging when we are fostering a bruised ego, drowning ourselves in a sea of disappointment or helplessness associated with the failure.

In order to learn from our failures, we first need to understand that it is okay if we feel ALL the emotions linked to failure for a short amount of time. Then, we need to get up and let it go by admitting the failure, such as: "Hey, you just failed" or "Hey, you made this big mistake". Now, during this process of letting it go, you need to grasp onto the "teachable moments" hidden within your failure.

You can't let failure stop you or you will never push yourself. Continue to push and test your limits because you believe in your vision, and success will follow. Let your experiences be an opportunity to grow and learn.

Ask yourself:

- What lesson does this failure have for me?
- How can I improve myself in case something similar were to happen again?

Go through your last plans and see where the fault was. Next, use your imagination to see how you would handle them differently if they ever came up again. Feel it as if you were there in that moment, experience the whole event and see yourself succeed.

LEARN from your mistakes and learn to laugh at them

Learning and laughter *can* and *should* work hand-in-hand. It's easier to learn something if you are enjoying the learning process, by accepting the fact that you might fail and being okay with it.

Your experiences and mistakes are the most effective way to learn because they create emotions. Life without emotion is dull and boring. So when you're excited, genuinely be and act excited. Don't be embarrassed or ashamed to feel the way you feel.

Laugh about the mistakes you once made. You can remember when you were a nervous wreck in a job interview, or when you completely choked when you tried to talk to that person you found very attractive, or when you were beet red as you were called in front of the class to answer a math equation. These events in your life certainly were embarrassing at the time, but the ability to laugh at them in retrospect is powerful and will give you fuel to keep moving forward. Smile now, and laugh.

Tony Robbins says it well with, "Go out and screw up. You're going to anyway so you might as well enjoy the process. Take the opportunity to learn from your mistakes; find the cause of your problem and eliminate it. Don't try to be perfect, just be an excellent example of being human."

PAIN MAKES you stronger

Pain strengthens you because it gives you the opportunity to learn from your mistakes. Even though sometimes it seems like the pain will never go away, there is always a light at the other end. With time, energy, and knowledge a broken soul will transform into a magnificent one, similar to when boxer Rocky Balboa was crushed by opponent Apollo Creed and years later came back to win an extraordinary rematch. Therefore, you've got to keep moving forward, day by day and minute by minute, second by second. Break it down into tiny pieces until you can look at your pain as part of the process of healing, and come up with an action plan filled with knowledge from various resources found on the internet. Resources such as self-help eBooks or videos on YouTube will help inspire you to move past your mistake.

With emotional pain, such as demeaning another person with yelling or name-calling, the callousness that often develops are walls of separation between you and the other person.

Cherry was sick of it. She was flooded with pain from the inside and it was beginning to show on the outside, as she begun to take eat fast foods, and limit her amount of exercise. Her boyfriend, Jake would complain and yell at her daily. Things such as, "You're so stupid! Why don't you just get a job and do something useful with your time?!" or *"You're so lazy! Why don't you stop watching TV and exercise instead!"*

Little did he know that each time the Jake hurt her, an invisible wall of distance got thicker, and pushed Cherry further away (making it very difficult to connect on an emotional level). She was bottling up this hurt inside, and it was showing on the outside. Interestingly enough, Jake didn't know he was doing anything wrong because that is how his father treated his mother.

Since you can't control another person's actions, there are two ways to overcome this pain such as:

- You can completely remove them from your life
- You can discover new ways to look at the situation by asking the person WHY they do the thing that causes you pain, and try to understand it. Is this person coming from a place of love or hate?

A NEW PERSPECTIVE

Another example could be if you made ten sales calls, feeling like a frustrated failure because you got rejected and hung up on nine out of ten calls. There are two ways you can look at this situation.

Jill felt like a failure at her job because nine out or ten sales calls were rejects. She wanted to quit her job because her perspective was that if she is obviously not good at her job if she can only have one successful sales call.

Liz had a different perspective. She believed that we live in a "world of abundance". She also went with the mindset that she had to make at least 10 calls for one to be a success. Therefore, she'd get on the call and as soon as she felt strong resistance, she made the decision to say, "It was great talking to you. Thank you for your time", and end the call.

The most important thing to do is not blame yourself because you should never feel like a failure. You are not a failure, you just had calls that failed. After all, maybe the person on the other line was having a horrible day. Maybe his or her dog just died, or had just got fired, or just got dumped.

However, you should look deep inside your heart and soul and find the will to forgive. Develop the willpower to smile or laugh at your past no matter how dark it seemed. For example, if your boss talked down to you when you made a mistake – making you feel less confident and quite emotionally and mentally weak in certain instances – it's necessary to look at that experience through different lenses. Maybe take the perspective of placing less importance on others' opinions about you.

Ask yourself:

- How would "a person you admire" look at your situation? What would they say about it? What advice would he or she give you?
- What if every time you looked at someone who intimidates you, such as your boss, you imagined a tiny pink mouse wearing a blue birthday hat on his nose?
- Imagine you're a fly on the wall twenty-feet away staring at yourself being human and making that mistake, what would you say about your situation?
- Imagine your life is a movie and you're the director who can visualize and dream up a new

scene so that you can see it from a new perspective. What does it look like?

You can dramatically lighten any situation by using your inner-child to create something that makes the situation seem comical and outlandish.

After a hard break-up, Jason was new to the dating world. He wanted to start meeting women and eventually find someone to love again. After reading several books on how to talk to women, he finally got the courage to do it. Even though he approached each woman in a respectful and friendly way, half of them either gave him a negative response or ignored him. He felt discouraged and gave up shortly afterwards because of the reactions he'd received.

A few weeks later he shifted his perspective. Instead of letting women's negative responses bring him down, he got excited about the fact that he was being courageous and talking to strangers with complete curiosity as if he were about to unwrap a new gift.

FORGIVE others

How willing are you to forgive *yourself* and *others* for the things that happened in the past? It is easier said than done, and you're not alone in this. Bitterness and grudges are amongst the things that primarily make up negative thoughts of the past. By replacing those feelings with forgiveness, love, and good memories toward those who have hurt or disappointed you, you unchain yourself from the anger and resentment of the past. This considerably makes letting go easier, as it will release the tension between you and your feelings toward the other person that you've been holding on to.

Sarah hated her dad for disconnecting himself from his family because of a drug addiction he had. She felt that he chose drugs over wanting to have a good relationship with her. When he tried to recon-

nect with her, she would avoid his calls and not answer the door when he'd ring the doorbell because she was holding on to this hatred and wasn't open to forgiveness. Whenever his name came up, the words that came to her mind were, "loser, betrayer, and addict".

Years had gone by and they still hadn't talked. One day she recognized that she was building a huge wall of resentment and stress that was unnecessary because she could not control her dad's actions. She knew that if she ever wanted to feel okay about her dad or have any relationship with him, she had to accept him for who he was and forgive him for what he'd done, or else this wall of resentment would forever remain.

When you choose to forgive and accept others, you're healing wounds. You're letting go of the past and giving yourself the ability to remain in the present moment when their name is brought up, instead of associating this person with only negative feelings.

When issues regarding trust arise, and extending forgiveness becomes seemingly impossible, take a look at the situation once again. Are you the one who's losing more in this silent and prolonged war? Are you the one who's wasting time and energy thinking of the loss instead of forgiving and moving on?

The present is the perfect time to mend wounds. Even though your past may seem to span hundreds of years, forgiveness can happen today. It is one of the keys that allow you to get "unstuck" and move forward in your life. If you're not going to forgive others, a joyful life in the present moment will be even further from your grasp. It's true that your relationship with these people may no longer be the same as before, but now is the perfect time to mend wounds – no matter how deep they are – and reignite a healthy relationship by simply forgiving and letting it go.

. . .

FORGIVE yourself

Forgiveness directed toward the self is much easier said than done since we as humans are both our best and worst critics. Therefore we expect the best of ourselves and tend to judge ourselves harshly if things fail to go as planned. How many times have you blamed yourself for a mistake that was completely out of your control? How many times have you missed opportunities because of your own fear and insecurities from past mistakes? What if you were to remove those memories, be fully present, and give yourself a clean slate? Think of how your life would be different if you approached every new challenging situation that way.

Forgiveness brings a new sense of freedom, a gentle unchaining of you from things of the past. It is not the same as forgetting a fault, but it's enough to push you forward to bring you closer to being fully present, and living a life that brings you joy. Hesitation to forgive yourself will limit your thoughts and actions. It's like having a cloudy mind that is blocking creativity, leaving you unable to think clearly.

Once you commit to forgiving yourself from the past, you can spread your own wings. You will begin to have a clear mind and feel a sense of inner peace. Others will begin to notice and feel a positive shift towards your energy when they are around you.

The fact is that you'll still make mistakes because you're human and you'll still get hurt because you have feelings. However, forgiveness enables you to be fully charged up to face new challenges because you've embraced the fact that you're simply human and you make mistakes.

Before you can extend forgiveness to others, you must start with yourself because it's hard to give something you don't have. Forgiveness can be looked at as closing chapters to the story of your life in which you've chosen to forgive yourself and others for mishaps.

Humans are not perfect. If we were then life would be boring because there would be no room for improvement or growth, and you wouldn't feel the joy of success that comes from hard work. Inevitably we will make mistakes and fail. It is one thing to take the blame and then give up, and it is another thing to take the blame and look for solutions to improve the situation for next time. Other times, things are out of your control, such as the weather conditions, other peoples' words and actions, or traffic on the freeway. Allow yourself forgiveness by telling yourself that it is okay to make mistakes because that is part of being human.

Imagine how life would be if everyone were to forgive each other for past mistakes, instead of hating or having a stale resentment toward each other.

Think of a past event that has been on your mind – one that has been consuming your energy and thoughts. Take a moment to relax and forgive yourself for what has happened. Take a deep breath and as you exhale, imagine light shades of smoke exiting your body as you send the past away. Next, take a moment to forgive others for what they have done to you so that you can unchain yourself from this hurt.

12

Seeing Past The Wildflowers

You can bring more of what you want into your life by focusing and constantly thinking about what you desire. Many people struggle at planning for the future because they don't know what they *truly* want in the next month, year, or five years.

What is it you truly want?

If you have a goal, don't just think about the end result of the goal. Feel the excitement associated with how it will *feel* to achieve that goal. While keeping that feeling in your mind, enjoy each of the small steps that are bringing you closer to your goal. Write out all the tiny steps it takes to achieve your goal, and the emotions you associate with each step such as *proud*, *accomplished*, or *successful*. This will be your motivation to keep making life better each day.

Put reminders in your environment that will remind you of that feeling so that it resonates within you when you look at them. These things could be anything from a vision board to a picture on your smart phone, or even a to-do list so that you are constantly thinking of your goal. Use your creativity to unleash the weapon that works best for you. Then it will manifest itself once you put in the work.

TIME KEEPS TICKING

Without reminders of our vision or reminders of past successes to give us a slight boost of energy when we need it, it is easy to get so caught up in life that we lose focus on what is important and get consumed by thoughts of self-doubt. Although failure has proven to make us feel helpless, passive, and forces us to believe that no matter how hard we try we will never succeed. There are things we can do to get past this feeling of helplessness.

After I had gotten the boot from grad school, I was miserable, depressed, and afraid I would never earn the $120,000 of student loans I owed. I needed something, anything, to lift me up and to give me hope and inspiration. In my depressed state, I felt like I wanted to curl up into a dark corner and never come out. All I wanted was to feel happy again.

I searched online for "ways to feel better about yourself", and a YouTube video came up called "Morning Ritual" by Stefan Pylarinos. While watching it, I felt inspired to get up and start making some changes. He talked about what he did every single morning to get excited every day of his life. I was ready and determined to get out of this depressed funk I had been in for months.

This showed me that everything I needed is within me, in the present moment; every single answer I needed was already there and I just needed to be in the right state of mind to access it.

The morning ritual started with taking a few minutes every single morning to smile, stretch, and take a few deep breaths to fill my lungs with oxygen; then it moved into something that really resonated with me – positive affirmations, which are simple reminders of the great qualities I already possessed, as well as qualities that I desired to have, and to feel grateful for each of them as if I'd already acquired them.

Next I created a vision board with things I wanted in the next three years. I used a bulletin board that I had used for one of my class projects – and found images from magazines of things that I wanted such as money to travel to see the world, pay back my student loans, and start a family someday. It also included pictures of people with disabilities and homeless people that I could help, as well as a fun, romantic relationship. Lastly, it gave me a list of empowering questions to ask myself every morning to help me choose what I wanted out of each precious day.

I was committed to taking an hour every morning to do exactly what the morning ritual video suggested, for a minimum of 30 days. When I first started the morning ritual, I felt silly and didn't want anyone to see me doing it. After 30 days I felt so good about myself that I wanted to share it with my family and friends because of the powerful effect it had on me. Overall, this routine showed me that if you focus on positive thoughts, you can attract more positive feelings to enrich your present moment. Most importantly, it got me out of a depressed, worthless mindset I'd felt for months and brought me to a happy place where I could begin to find direction in life.

The next time you make a new plan for achieving something in the future – even if you've already failed at it once, make sure to plan it with a fresh start, removing the previous faults, and using positive thoughts to attract positive feelings. Most importantly, while on your journey to reach your goal, live in the present moment, remembering to make the process of reaching the goal an enjoyable one. One step at a time, day-by-day, not day to month.

PSYCHOLOGICAL MOMENTUM

In psychology, there is a phenomenon called "psychological momentum", in which success breeds success, and failure breeds failure. It begins with the basic laws of physics that Newton discovered, explaining that momentum equals velocity times mass. Whereas psychological velocity spikes with an important event, such as when the officiant tells the groom that he may kiss the bride, or when a football player makes a huge interception. The greater the emotional importance of the event is, the greater the mass. When the mass is combined with velocity, momentum is produced.

It is the effect of these compelling feelings that our minds and bodies lose momentum due to past failures and we believe we won't succeed further, so we give up. However, it is possible to quickly overcome these negative emotions after a failure, by focusing on things which we can control, such as our action to getting back up and trying again until you succeed. In addition, it is okay to ask for help because we as humans are designed to help each other. Each of us were given gifts that are unique to each individual on earth. Often times we can't do it on our own. You can use your gift to help others who are lacking, and vise versa.

Be proactive by taking action now. Make the most of what you have, and enhance your skills *now*, not one month from now. The present moment is the moment you can transition from the stickiness of past mistakes, and shoot up to the clear blue skies of clarity and purpose that your future holds.

PATIENCE IS a golden process

You shouldn't force things to happen. The problem with the human subconscious mind is that it is like a spring: the more you push it, the more it will push you back. Sometimes, you just have to be patient and enjoy the waiting process, no matter how bad you want something or how hard you work to make it happen. You can't just sow a seed today and take it out every day to see if any branch, or fruit has sprouted. If you keep faith in your purpose, and patiently keep watering the seed, you will see it grow.

Daniel had a dream. His dream was to start his own business because he wanted the freedom to work at his own pace, not at one that his boss demanded. He also dreamt of having a passive income so that he could pursue his passion of traveling around the world and learning about all types of cultures. He got his break when he attended a lecture on "How to become financially free".

The type of business he wanted to start was an online Book Publishing business, in which he could get started fairly inexpensively and begin to get payments whenever the books he published were sold. Although, initially he only had $1,000 to invest in his business, he knew that if he was willing to take this leap, he would have to be patient and keep investing the money that he earned back into the business in order for it to grow. He felt in his heart that if he kept putting his focus, time, and energy into this business that he would reap the benefits.

Daniel quit his job after entering the Kindle Publishing business after six months. Three months after that, he had made a total of only $3,000. However, each month his royalties had doubled and he trusted that his monthly income would continue to grow as he published more high quality books. He was inspired to continue publishing books and use his time wisely, spending hours each day learning how to be most efficient with the Kindle Publishing business. Most importantly, he had patience and believed that the rewards for the hard work would pay off.

After 18 months of repeating the process, he was making $15,000 each month. He was incredibly grateful for his patience and willingness to take the leap and start his own business. Now, he is traveling the world, working in coffee shops (with internet access), and not having to be bossed around by anyone besides himself.

Happiness

Imagine if you were to fully embrace each moment, and not worry or stress about the future because you have placed the future where it belongs – in the back of your mind, or on a vision board, or on your goal list, but still being fully aware of your goal.

Imagine if you were to formulate a road map, laying out each of the steps to get you to your goal. Take one day at a time so that you can live in the present moment, being fully aware of the beautiful colors that you can see, the taste of the moist air, the texture of the chair you're sitting on, the sounds of the birds chirping, and the excitement you feel in this moment. What if you were to keep *what is going on in the present moment* at the forefront of your mind? Think about that for a minute.

You might be amazed at the little details that you begin to observe by taking life at a slower pace so that you can fully experience the present moment. Life may seem short, and if you are constantly worried about your future, you'll feel anxious and unsatisfied because you'll feel like there is always more you need to be doing. However, if you can set a goal and focus on the outcome with 10% of your energy, and allow yourself to be fully engaged in the present moment with each task at hand, you'll not only do a more efficient job (as opposed to multitasking), but you'll also be able to feel and take in the joy of the present moment as you get closer to your goal.

If you are constantly worried about your future, you'll feel anxious and unsatisfied because you'll feel like there is always more you need to be doing. Set a goal and focus on the outcome with 10% of your energy, use another 10% to reflect on your past mistakes to improve your success rate, and allow yourself to be 80% engaged in the present moment with each task you do. You'll not only do a more efficient job but you'll also be able to feel and take in the joy of the present moment as you get closer to your goal.

THE ROAD ahead

Trust that you are on the right path. Work smarter, not harder. Enjoy the journey, not only the outcome. Escape the fears and worries of the mind and enjoy the process, by living and breathing the present moment. If the goal is the only focus you might burn out or lose interest. It is key to enjoy the process so that your goal doesn't feel overwhelming or unreachable.

COMBINING mistakes and the future with the present moment

Acknowledging your mistake is the first and the most crucial step towards learning from your mistakes and failures. You may be the type of person who blames circumstances for a setback. In this case, it is difficult to mold and grow because by placing the blame on someone or something else, you are saying it is out of your control and that there is nothing you can do to improve the situation. Of course there are instances where it is out of your control, but this is not always the case. It is challenging to be able to enjoy the present moment if your happiness depends upon the outcomes of situations or circumstances. If you admit your mistakes, and hold yourself responsible for the failure, you regain the power. In doing so, don't be hard on yourself, simply be aware that something needs to change.

Admitting mistakes and apologizing is often challenging at first because it often causes feelings of guilt, embarrassment, or shame. However, it is also freeing and those painful feelings won't last long if you admit to your mistake. At this point, you can use the power of being in the present moment to change your current reality of feeling like a failure, to one of being a successful person in whichever field you desire.

Megan was a nurse who absolutely loved engaging in meaningful conversations with each of her patients, and was seen by many as the "mother-nurse" who would go above and beyond her duties for each of her patients. However, she had a tendency to get flustered and nervous due to the fast pace in the medical world, which caused her to make minor mistakes on the job, such as not fully completing reports which upset the doctors and other team members. She recognized that she was often in a future-mindset when writing these reports, thinking of what she needed to do next, and missing out on what was truly important in that moment – completing the reports.

Megan knew she'd get fired if she did not do something about the reports. It was suggested that she be more in the present moment when writing the reports, similar to the way she'd have loving conversations with the patients she worked with in which her eyes, ears, and heart were fully engaged.

Megan implemented the suggestion and chose to be patient with herself, and be fully engaged and aware of the present moment – not worrying about things she had to do five minutes from then or the mistakes she'd made in the past. She even informed each of her co-workers that she intended to be more in the present moment when writing the reports. She would sit down to write the report and imagine herself in a big box and the only things inside the box were her mind, her body, the pen, the report, the table she was writing on, and the chair she was sitting on – keeping these things her primary focus. She would normally be multitasking as she would work with two patients at a time, however, when the report was in front of her, she completed it.

Interestingly enough, she feared she wouldn't have enough time to complete the report, and when all was said and done she completed the report faster than before because her thoughts and actions were fully present, as opposed to worrying about what she had to do next.

Knowing and understanding this gives you the ability to completely *listen* to what is being said, or fully enjoy the *taste* of a meal or the *sound* of a piece of music. When we multitask in our heads, for instance planning a trip while studying some important information, we are not enjoying the present moment, nor are we giving our best to the two tasks. "Any man," says Albert Einstein, "who can drive safely while kissing a pretty girl is simply not giving the kiss the attention it deserves."

ANOTHER PERSPECTIVE

Most of the problems between you and another person resolve when you understand the other person's perspective. It is like seeing the world with a shiny new pair of glasses. Therefore take the time to put yourself in another person's shoes.

There is no need to get embarrassed by publicly confessing your mistakes, but you need to be true to yourself by taking credit of your mistakes in order to learn from them. Also, you don't need to condemn yourself as a failure, in fact you should think of failure as a stepping-stone for climbing onto the ladder of success.

Sam had a secret. He was addicted to pornography. He felt that it was consuming his thoughts and taking over his life, as if he were a prisoner to pornography. He didn't want to tell anyone because he was embarrassed of what his wife Cindy would think, and possibly divorce him. He was letting anxiety get the best of him.

Little did he know that if he openly communicated with Cindy about his problem they could figure something out together. Instead, Sam grew more distant and their relationship began to suffer – especially sexually. Cindy had a feeling that there was something Sam wasn't telling her. She wanted to understand what Sam was going through, and help him overcome it so that their relationship could smooth out again.

After Cindy repeatedly questioned Sam about his issue, he opened up to her and stated that he wasn't satisfied sexually so he began looking at pornography. He claimed that it was easy, fast, and didn't require any effort. Cindy was furious – not so much about the pornography addiction – but more so that he had kept it a secret for months, allowing their relationship to suffer.

Sam felt guilty for not being open with his communication and she wanted to understand why Sam wanted to look at porn. After discussing it, the bottom line was that Sam wasn't making love to his wife as much as he desired. Therefore, instead of initiating sex, he settled to watching porn, which ultimately wasn't fulfilling for him. He felt as if he were falling down a tunnel and continued the downward spiral. He learned that his wife always wanted him to pursue her whenever he was feeling sexual.

Sam felt relieved after admitting his addiction to porn and he knew in his heart that there were thousands, if not millions of men who were suffering from a similar situation. Therefore, he put himself on blast by sharing his situation with all his friends on Facebook, and they shared it with their friends. This was a way of not only showing a vulnerable side of himself so that it could help many other families, but also a way of holding himself accountable to openly communicating with his wife about their sexual relationship.

Start evaluating where anxiety and fear is eating at you. What can you implement today to relieve your feelings of anxiety? Is there a person you can talk to that will make the anxious feeling fade away? Once you resolve these issues, and remove the anxious feelings, your present moment will feel clear and easier to access.

What is something you are currently worrying about? Think about whether you can control it or not. Imagine if you were to be open about your feelings and share it with a loved one so that they can understand your worry. How important is it for you to hold onto this worry? Are you ready to let it go?

13

A Brighter Future

Insurance companies thrive due to the fact that most people are concerned about their future. People want to prevent feelings of worry about not being protected in case a catastrophic event were to happen. Therefore, it is wise to have something prepared in case you have an accident. Once you have insurance in place, it will allow you to feel safe, have peace of mind, and bring you back to the present moment.

THE FUTURE IS NOT controllable

If you believe in a higher being or a deity, you'll claim that only God, Allah, or some other higher power can control what happens in the future. If you don't adhere to any religious beliefs, you'll still probably think that controlling the future is impossible. You can't control what will be on the front page of the news or if you'll win a million dollars in a Las Vegas slot machine a week from now. The only thing you can control is the present and even this period is limited to what's within your reach.

If you live in the future, you will often feel anxious. You'll feel different states of anxiety such as nervousness and excitement. You may be excited about a bonus check that your expecting in the mail. You may be excited about a new album that will be released tomorrow. The flip side is that if you choose to live in the future world, you will commonly experience feelings of nervousness and fear. For example, if you were to go on a job interview tomorrow, you may be nervous about how it will go. The fastest way to alleviate this worry is to take action.

Use the present moment to do what it takes to get prepared. Instead of staying in a state of fear, seek out the things the position entails. Visualize and feel how you can be a unique asset to the company, and do a mock interview with a friend.

Many worries stem from things that are out of your control. For example, you may worry about getting old. This is something you have absolutely no control over because time is unstoppable. You can influence how old you feel by eating healthy, exercising, and surrounding yourself around positive people. If you're so worried about getting old, you'll miss out on living the life you are given. Embrace your age. If you're 50, embrace being 50, and make it the best year ever. Believe that each year will be better than the next.

Worries naturally occur in most people, but you can train yourself to not overwhelm yourself by obsessing over them. Concentrate on living in the present moment, taking one minute at a time. Use your energy and abilities to make the present a better one. Thinking about the future and trying to control it will only zap your joy.

THE FUTURE IS **unpredictable**

You cannot control the future because you cannot predict it. Many people go to fortune-tellers or to people who claim they can foresee what's going to happen. No matter how many years of experience someone has in developing his or her self-claimed "gifts" of predicting the future, nothing is set in stone.

Remember that your plans and goals for the future are still written in sand. They can be washed away by the circumstances that you will eventually face; they can be altered by other factors such as changes in your desires or realizations regarding your purpose in life. You honestly can't predict exactly what you're going to do tomorrow or what your boss will tell you regarding your job.

You are not sure what the future holds. No matter how long people try to think about it, predictions about the future will remain what they are – prophecies, guesses, forecasts... you name it! As you let go of your past due to the realization that you *can't* change it, remember that despite the unpredictability of the future, you *can* still change what it may become if you focus on living well in the present.

THE FUTURE IS NOT the enemy

Generally, people are good at being pessimistic and they love to exaggerate many possible circumstances in their lives. Thoughts such as, "I won't be able to graduate from college because Advanced Chemistry is so hard," represent only a small part of what people – particularly the relatively young ones – are worried about. Some people may even think that they won't be able to meet a great person to marry because they'd been looking and they hadn't been able to find one. Others are primarily concerned about their career and they think that they'll just be stuck in whatever position they're in because they lack the necessary skills and knowledge to move up the ladder.

The future has become a common enemy of many individuals and this is clearly unhelpful and unnecessary because the future doesn't have any sides. It's neither for the bad nor the good. It doesn't have a will of its own, so it can't actually plot any evil scheme against you. It's just an unpredictable period of time and is determined by the actions and choices we make in the present.

In most cases, though, the future is not as bad as you think it'll be. Once you're there in the interview room, you realize that you're able to answer the employer's questions with confidence and certainty. Once you submit that carefully written project or paper, you'll see that your teacher appreciates the hard work that's clearly in how meticulously you accomplished the assignment. Once you're in the exam room, you'll see most of the questions about chemicals and compounds are not gibberish, but can actually be answered if careful calculations and considerations are made.

WHAT YOU'RE EXPECTING to happen will most likely happen

Remember that what you're expecting to happen will most likely happen if you've invested significant amount of energy into thinking that things will unfold in such a way. As Rhonda Byrne says in *The Secret*, "Your thoughts become things." If you expect the worst, the worst may materialize itself.

Some use the present to soothe the future with visualization techniques. For example, visualizing being at an interview and experiencing how it would feel to be there, what the interviewer might ask you and how you'd like to respond will ease anxiety and tension.

As Allyson Felix, the 2012 Olympic Gold Medalist said, "I am a big believer in visualization. I run through my races mentally so that I feel even more prepared." It's once again about choice. You'll see what you want to see, and even though you can't predict the future, using the present to visualize will surely decrease anxiety and worry for the future.

The future is not your enemy. It is dependent on what you're doing at the moment; so stop worrying about it because these efforts are pointless. Take action now, and embrace your fears to overpower feelings of anxiety and worry.

HEALTHY PLANNING for the future

No one's telling you to stop preparing for the future altogether, but *thinking* and *worrying* about it are clearly two different things. You can plan for your future in a healthy way, which won't cause you to get sucked into a seemingly inescapable cycle of worry, disappointment, fear, and sorrow.

As mentioned previously, one thing that I've found very useful is having the Present consume 80% of my thoughts and feelings, with the Past taking up 10%, and the Future being the other 10%. Of course, this can't be an exact measurement, but it is a good ballpark figure that works to remain present, while still being aware of the past and future.

LETTING GO of the reins

Most families start saving money for the future. Saving

money is a healthy way of managing current wealth so that there's money for a highly probable future, including college, retirement, or an overseas vacation. As you can see, there are ways you can prepare for the future without stressing over each and every detail. You should not *worry* about what degree your child will get or what type of people he'll meet in college because these are uncontrollable factors. You can influence his decisions in college, but ultimately it is his choice.

Another example that causes stress and worry is watching the evening news. The majority of the things on the news will not and do not affect us, but instead cause anxiety and worry for the future, which again is not under our control. We can attempt to prevent terrorist attacks or getting burglarized, however, there is only so much you can do because you cannot control other people's actions. If something comes up that is important to us, we will hear about it through social media (Facebook, Twitter, Email, Google, Yahoo, the list goes on), or through word of mouth.

What is something you are currently worrying about? Think about whether you can control it or not. How important is it for you to hold onto this worry?

For the next week, my request is for you to give yourself permission to let go of this worry. Whenever it comes up, jump back into the present and focus on your breathing. If you need reminders (e.g. sticky notes, a piece of jewelry, or adding it to your daily calendar, etc.) go ahead and put those in place. Commit to letting go of the worry.

In one week, check back in and see how that worry is. How did it feel when you weren't worrying about it? What's changed since letting go of that worry?

14

Your New Gift

Imagine a giant jigsaw puzzle of the world with each mineral, plant, animal, and human each representing a beautiful piece of the puzzle. Without one another, the puzzle would not fit. The world simply would not work. It's the contrasts that make life so vibrant and colorful. By embracing the world's differences, we can reveal a new world beyond the curtains – one in which we've never seen, heard, or felt. It is a new world, an undiscovered world that very few have lived in. It is the present moment and its dynamic beauties are well worth discovering.

It's the ability to coexist in an uncertain world that keeps life interesting. In order to survive, we must coexist. We must embrace our differences and be enlightened by the strengths of others in order to bring more happiness to our lives. The world was designed to be one that is shared – all the natural resources, as well as the resources that were made from man (who created the resources from things from the earth). This philosophy is not the norm – it's not that most people are selfish and only think of themselves, instead it's because that's how humans have been trained to think.

The people who choose to push against the current and resist the norms, are the ones who add the brightest color to life. We as humans are designed to think in the past or the future. However, it is the present moment in which we are most productive. It is in the present moment that we can connect and are fully engaged in meaningful conversations. The present moment is where we can fully taste our foods to every sliver of chew.

You are given a choice to live in the present moment. Doing so diminishes the power of fear, and moves people past the feelings of depression. To be completely in the present is to see the world as a beautiful, colorful place, filled with possibilities, as opposed to a black and white world with limited options. It has the power to give you a fresh start, erasing the sabotaging voices of the past that have been holding you back.

Once you enter the land of the present moment, you leave all previous judgments, worries, and fears behind as you engage in conversation. You will speak from a place of curiosity, wonder, and amazement, as opposed to worrying about what you should say next. It transforms lives from a blue and sad existence into an exciting, more meaningful one.

For years, my friends and peers perceived me as a good listener, even though I wasn't. I would give great eye contact and the occasional head nods to make it appear that I comprehending everything that was being said. If the speaker asked me to repeat or explain what was being said, I wasn't able to because I was thinking about either what I should say next, or something like how amazing it would be to eat an apple pie right now. I couldn't focus because I did not understand how to be in the present moment.

Since then I've learned that connecting with others on an

emotional level and truly understanding what another individual is saying is one of the most incredible things that we as humans can do – and we can only do it if we are in the present moment, taking in the person's words, tone of voice, and every individual meaning behind the words. We are giving another person the precious gift of not only our time, but also our ears for listening and our feelings for understanding. In exchange, we receive the gift of understanding how strange, confusing, and beautiful humans are.

People are limited to the amount of things they can do with the amount of time they are given on earth. There is always something more that each person wants once they begin entering a future mindset because of the fear of lack of time. Therefore, we try and exceed these limitations by multitasking. Many people think they're good at multitasking, but eventually learn that some things just *can't* be done simultaneously. For example, if you are attempting to have an engaging conversation on the phone and listening intently, while checking and reading your email, you are missing out on the experience of both because neither will have your full attention. You will miss details, and the quality of both will be diminished.

You can't focus on the present and fully see its beauty if you're too hung-up on the past or worried about the future. Essentially, you can't completely enjoy the *gift of the present* if you're filled with regret and worry. Imagine trying to listen to a friend telling you about the incredible time she had last night while thinking or imagining what type of pizza you are craving for dinner. You're either here, in the present moment engaging in the conversation, or you're in the future dreaming about your pizza. You may grasp the idea of the story, but you are missing out on the energy, the tone of voice, the words, and most importantly the meaning behind and between the words. The thoughts of your pizza can wait because it is difficult to let your curiosity roam (which is key to an engaging conversation) if your mind is not involved in the conversation.

Ever since Mark was a child he'd had difficulty paying attention to what people said. People would assume that he had Attention Deficit Disorder. As an adult he was ready for a change. He committed to being fully engaged and experience one conversation at a time. His technique was to compartmentalize his non-related conversation thoughts in his head. Hence during a conversation, once he began to recognize that he was stepping out of the present moment, he would take that thought and place it into his memory (or another compartment in his mind to access later) and then jump back into the moment saying, "I'm sorry, I missed that. Could you repeat what you just said?" Nevertheless, he had to be patient and consistent with himself during this process until he made it a habit of speaking in the present moment.

Imagine if you were to take each conversation, second by second, so that you were fully *there* and totally listening. How much more information could you retain? Would you be able to create more meaningful conversations, and talk for as long as you desire? How about if you were to add your intuition to that, and follow the tone of voice from the speaker? Could you understand what the person is *really* saying?

THE ILLUSION of time

Eckhart Tolle, the author of the widely recognized book, *Power of Now* stated, "Observe that the future is usually imagined as either better or worse than the present. If the future is better, it gives you hope or pleasurable anticipation. If it is worse, it creates anxiety. Both are illusions." It's easy for people to think about or remember the past and try to predict the future, but only few allot a portion of their day to stop and think of where they are in the moment. It is also easy for people to imagine the worst possibility of a situation and be consumed by it, instead of taking a second to stop and place their thoughts and feelings in the present moment.

The beauty of life is in the present moment – the silence, the sound of the cars roaring their engines as they drive by, the music from the birds chirping, the voices from people in the distance, the feeling of the wind brushing against your face and gently pushing your hair to one side, the feeling of sunshine pressing against half of your body while the other half is covered with shade from an oak tree, the feeling of your heart beating inside your chest, the energy and feelings received from the person you are listening to as you're keenly listening to each word and the meaning behind each word. There is so much to be seen, heard, and felt in the present moment. My request for you is to stop for a few minutes to take it all in.

The present may only be explained using the definition of the past and the future, even though it's quite detached from the other two time periods – it is the space between. It is the space in which changes can be made; the space of new beginnings; the space in which your body will forever remain. If the mind and the body are aligned in the present moment, you are totally in the present. To overcome the illusion of time and realize that you're more than the sum of your past and the predictions of your future, you must first be aware of the power of thoughts and feelings inside your mind that can instantly change your body.

I had five minutes until I had to give a business presentation on the impact of Solar Energy and how it can positively impact our world. I was very nervous and had fearful thoughts racing through my head. What if I forget what I learned over the past week of researching solar energy? What if people aren't interested? What if my mind goes blank? What if I run out of things to say? What if I can't answer a question from the audience?

All these thoughts were bringing me into a state of anxiety, and I felt like my presentation was going to flop. Then, with only two minutes until I was up, I stood up straight, pulled my shoulders back, took a deep breath to fill my lungs, and forced a smile. A rush of excitement flowed through my body and relaxed my mind, bringing me back into the present moment. I took one more deep breath and stopped thinking about what I was going to say, and felt grateful for having the opportunity to speak in front of so many people to share this important information.

Once you see the beauty of the present moment – the only reality that ever exists, you won't be submerged in anxiety of the future, or guilt from past mistakes.

LIVING in an illusion

Mitch Albom wrote a very inspiring and thought-provoking novel entitled "The Time Keeper." In this book, he illustrated through his words the pitfalls of being overly concerned about time and counting the seconds instead of living them. The three main characters in the novel suffered much because of their attachment to time, but were able to find salvation in the end by realizing that what's important is to enjoy each and every second of your life doing what you can and should do, and spending your life with the ones you love.

Years ago, people lived simply and were quite happy because instead of being concerned of the time lost, they focused on the time they still had; the time they could use to improve themselves and be a positive contribution to society. Many of the greatest inventions in history were created because of pioneers and inventors who chose to live in the present and not linger in past mistakes or worry much about the future.

Thomas Edison had to try many materials and had to face numerous failures before he was able to invent the incandescent light bulb. Alexander Graham Bell failed at several things including the "flying machine", before inventing the telephone. What if these brilliant men only focused on their past failures and mistakes?

You get closer to your goal by focusing on the tasks at hand. Look into the present and do not worry about how your past still clings to a part of your identity or how your future will unfold one day. When you're immersed in the present, this present will eventually be a wonderful memory of the past and will be the catalyst to creating a better future.

LISTEN to your life

One of the reasons most people have a hard time *living in the present* is because they are too busy talking, over-analyzing, and thinking. Only few have actually developed great listening skills, enabling them to see, feel, and absolutely understand what they have before them. As many leaders claim, those who listen gain more than those who talk.

People love talking about themselves. There is a difference between listening to someone speak and actually being with someone, fully engaged and absorbing the information coming from their lips. This includes more than empathizing. It is connecting, feeling, seeing and experiencing what is behind and between the person's words in that present moment.

If you can put on a hat filled with curiosity, then instead of holding the questions in your mind, you can just

Happiness

be present with the other person and let the questions naturally flow in the conversation. The trick is to listen and be curious about the words, tone of voice, and digging deep to determine what the person is *really* trying to say by asking open-ended questions. Simply by using this method of curiosity and being in the present moment, you will have conversations that will last for hours, and the other person will love you for it. It will take practice, but once you understand how to apply it by doing it repetitively, you will feel the powerful effects in all your interactions. For more information on this subject, I encourage you to take a look at one of my books that goes into detail on how to have amazing conversations with anyone. It's titled: Do Talk To Strangers.

Cindy was on a quest to find the man of her dreams. She went on a lot of dates and had a hard time finding a connection with any man. Even though most people found her attractive with her long brown hair and beautiful brown eyes, she rarely went on a 2nd or 3rd date because the connection was not there. She took an outside look at her dating life, and played a few dates back in her head. She concluded that she was talking all about herself, and not asking curious questions of the other person. It's not that she didn't want to ask questions, she just didn't know what to ask.

For her future dates, she decided to try something new – to enter the date from a mindset of "curiosity in the present moment". Therefore, she would engage in the conversation and not be the one answering all the questions, but instead be engaged in conversation by being curious about her dates' words, actions, and the environment. After doing this, she noticed that she learned a lot more about her dates and could weed out the ones she didn't like based on their energies, and even the type of words used, noticing if they had a more positive or negative tone to them. She had a lot more fun speaking from a place of curiosity and often experienced the feeling that time does not exist.

When living in the present moment, you will begin to

notice how your listening skills significantly improve. You may begin to notice how fast time flies by as you're having hours of conversations that seem like only minutes. Your ability to connect and understand people will be taken to a new level, as you begin to hear people say, "I feel like I've known you my whole life."

Living in the present requires an understanding of *who you are* in this moment and *where your life is* right now. Since you are no longer focused on the passing of time — what the past has offered and what the future has in store — develop the habit of giving yourself alone time to listen to yourself to learn about your own life, without any outside influence.

You won't be able to listen to yourself if you're in the middle of the heavy traffic, in a crowded market, or while working. As discussed earlier in the section, it's important for you to set a "quiet time"; a time where you can absorb the silence and concentrate on becoming sensitive to your own emotional, mental, and even spiritual needs. Often times, people take their quiet time and find peace when connecting with nature. You can try hiking, or taking a walk outside breathing in the fresh air, or simply sitting outside under a willow tree.

As you sit in silence, notice your breathing patterns and what your body is telling you. Where are your hands? How are your legs feeling? How is your posture? Take a look inside yourself and think of all the amazing muscles, bones, and joints that make your body what it is, and allow it to move in so many directions. The silence will allow you to explore what you normally can't access in the midst of the noise and turmoil.

Once you choose to listen to yourself through meditation, you are choosing to be more aware of the present moment and will discover beautiful things within your subconscious mind. The silence will place thoughts and feelings that will drift in and out of your mind, including ones you may never have been aware of.

A JOURNEY of self-awareness

What if you were to take a week and spend it in complete silence? Perhaps in nature, such as Joshua Tree National Park, and record every single thought and feeling you had for the entire week. It sounds like quite a process, considering the human mind has thousands of thoughts throughout the day. I encourage you to give yourself the time to do this because it can be an eye-opening experience, a way of revealing and connecting with emotions that have been buried underneath your skin, bringing them to the surface. You may discover natural human emotions that you may have been denying for many years such as feelings of jealousy, guilt, greed, excitement, and peace.

Once you record all the thoughts and emotions you are experiencing, you can look back at your notes on the journey of self-awareness and be more in touch with your emotions in the present moment. Once you can master this, and immediately name your emotions while you're feeling them, you have power to fully feel the emotions and then let them go in order to move forward, and remain in the present moment.

A person's motives are made up of a mixture of the mind and the heart. For example, questions such as: Should I marry this person? Should I choose this degree for my University study? Should I have an abortion? Should I leave a day later so I can explore this beautiful city I am in? Of course, many of these questions are based on values, morals, and what you believe you *should* do based on your past experiences. If there were a way to directly link the power of the mind and the beauty of the heart, life would be far less complicated and decisions would be much easier. But there isn't, so you have to embrace the situation. Sometimes you have to go with your gut-feeling or intuition in the moment instead of battling between the heart and the mind.

UNNECESSARY IMAGINING and **conceptualizing**

People love to plan; and planners are particularly in high demand toward the end of each year to the first quarter of the following year. Many people use their smart phones to take note of reminders, meetings, and other activities so that they won't forget their responsibilities and commitments. You can say that a significant portion of people's time is spent planning for things; setting deadlines, parties, and other events.

The amazing thing about technology is that by having digital calendars, such as Google Calendars, it allows people to be more fully present. For example, if you have an appointment next week, or just remembered that you have a dinner party to go to tomorrow, you can use your smart phone or tablet to jot down the event. This way you will not have to worry about having to remember this event so that you can get it off your mind. You'll be able to enjoy where you are and the person you are with *in the moment*.

OVER-PLANNING your life away

The younger generations are particularly prone to such a planning frenzy. Those who are entering college and those who are about to head off to join the corporate world are fond of planning. It is understandable because fantasizing and dreaming about the future is exciting.

However, there are several disadvantages of *excessive planning*, and one of them is to *miss out on what's currently happening in your life*. Let's say you're on a business trip, and even while you're on the trip, you've already started thinking and planning for another one the following week, missing out on the entire experience.

If you constantly plan, imagine, or conceptualize your life, you will feel anxious and often overwhelmed with the amount of things you are planning for the future. Of course, planning for the future is important, but when it becomes excessive, you miss out on living in the present. Going back to the algorithm I use, only 10% of your life should be future- based, where you plan out steps for the action you will take in the present – consisting of 80%, and of course the lessons from the past makes up the other 10%. Remember, that life is one big journey and it should not be filled with plans that only eventually become a distraction for another plan.

After all, what you're ultimately looking for is joy and happiness, right? These come from a sense of accomplishment; a feeling that you've done your best to achieve your goal and have subsequently helped yourself and others. Plans mean nothing unless action is taken. They are just one of the steps to achieving your goals, which again comes from making a plan, and then being fully present when taking action.

ENJOY the present

Even though more than a couple of babies are born every second around the globe, many parents still suffer from losing a child due to miscarriages and illnesses that particularly target premature babies. Someone dies every second, either from accidents, murders, suicide, or terminal illnesses. These are examples of how short life can be and a reminder of how important it is to enjoy what you have right now, the present.

Not everyone is given the privilege of spending every day with loved ones. Many have to watch their husbands or fathers leave every year to serve in the army; to serve the nation. Others have work obligations that require spouses to be across the globe for a few weeks or months each year. Some people don't even get to spend more than a few years with their family and friends due to tragic accidents. The point is to cherish the moments you do have with loved ones because you never know if you will see them tomorrow, and the only lasting thing you have are memories – which, if fully tuned into the present moment, can last a lifetime.

You can't control the future and you can't change the past. No matter how much people want it, you can't predict what will happen in the next few seconds, minutes, hours, days, weeks, months, or years. There are things that are beyond your control not because life's punishing you, but because it wants you to see that the unpredictability and the fragility of your existence makes life that much more precious. Every second becomes more beautiful because it may be the last, so soak it in.

If you're still unsure of what you should do to fully enjoy the present because you're still in the process of letting go of the past, or perhaps you are training yourself to stop worrying about the future. Moving on from the past may require a longer time than you think, but it's not exactly a process that should be rushed. It may require more than a couple of nights' efforts to fully commit to living in the present, but keep moving forward because the internal rewards are astounding.

Now, think of all the things you have to get done today, and tomorrow, and the rest of this week. How many thoughts are racing though your mind right now? How many times a day do you attempt to do several things at once?

My request for you is to go *one day without multitasking*, to experience it. This is not to decrease your productivity, but instead to see the beauty in every single thing you do. Often times, you will be more productive and far more efficient when you take the moment to do just one thing at a time.

Be fully immersed in the one activity you are doing, without being distracted. For example, if you are having a conversation at lunch and your cell phone buzzes, don't text or answer the phone (or simply keep your phone on silent); for each food you eat actually *taste it* instead of viewing Facebook or text messages on your phone; or even if you are doing a chore, for instance the laundry, be fully immersed in the activity using your senses in the present moment – instead of thinking about what happened earlier that day or what else you need to be doing. Think about the smell in the air, the texture of the clothes, feel how your arms move when you're placing the laundry in the washing machine. Be in the moment.

You may find this request completely ridiculous or you may find it absolutely refreshing, but either way you won't know what it is like until you experience it. So, go ahead and try it, just for a day.

15

Perpetual Happiness

Dreams, goals, and New Year resolutions are powerful components to a fulfilling life. Without goals, you would have feel like a leaf in the wind, simply drifting and watching life pass by you before your eyes. They give direction to life and allow the present moment to be more meaningful by giving it purpose. Although goals are important, we need not be so consumed with goals that we miss out on the joys and beauties of life in the present moment. Goals act as an internal compass giving us direction to how we need to spend our time in the present moment. We need them to grow into stronger people than we were yesterday.

Sarah was caught up in the daily cycle of attending medical school, then studying whenever she was not in class. She was constantly focused on her end goal of becoming a doctor. After year three, she began to feel overwhelmed and impatient with how long it was taking to get through med school, and the five more years she had to go. Her grades began to drop, as she was only focused on the end result, how hard she was working, and how long it was taking. She was not absorbing the process of taking each class one day at a time.

She began to lose interest in the classes and as a result she'd miss some of them. If she didn't make changes, she wouldn't ever reach her goal of becoming a doctor, and be disappointed in herself, thus feeling like a failure.

Sarah took a semester off, as she wanted to take time for herself and get realigned with why she wanted to become a doctor in the first place. After all, she didn't want all the time, energy, and money to go to waste if she wasn't truly passionate about becoming a doctor. During this time, she discovered her life purpose, which was to bring light to other's lives by inspiring and helping other people every day. This resonated with her and every day she reminded herself of the purpose she was becoming a doctor. She wore her purpose every day, keeping it in her heart with every class she attended, and every activity she participated in.

Many people struggle with working towards their goals because they are focused only on the end result, as opposed to taking each day one step at a time and enjoying the process. Of course, not everything will be a pleasurable experience but you aren't anywhere other than where you are supposed to be – living and breathing in the present moment.

Fear of the unknown is a roadblock that causes people to live a life without any direction, by allowing life to drift away by not taking action when opportunities present themselves in your mind or your environment. Thus, taking one step at a time without worrying about your next steps will allow you to enjoy the present moment. If your dream is to start a business, or to find a lasting relationship, or to find a career you enjoy, then don't put your energy into your worry (the fear of the unknown), instead accept where you are in life, and get excited about the small action-steps that will bring you closer to your goal.

. . .

REWARDS ON MILESTONE completion

It is key to set mini-goals. For instance, if your goal needs to be accomplished one month down the road, have accomplishment rewards each week so that after you finish a milestone or get a good deal of success by achieving your mini-goal on time, reward yourself with something you like. This may be something as simple as eating a frozen yogurt, watching your favorite TV show or movie, planning a trip or hang out with friends/family. The more you reward yourself on completing each goal, the more consistent and productive you'll be.

Mark was 29 years old and had never been in a serious relationship. He joked around that he was like the character played by Steve Carrell in the movie titled 40-Year Old Virgin. As a computer programmer, working at a large successful company, he felt like life was good, apart from his romantic life. Therefore, he was ready for change and committed to setting goals and wanted me to hold him accountable.

In addition, each day before he went out to socialize, he took a few minutes to visualize, or to imagine himself achieving the goal from start to finish. Being a rather shy and introverted person, he knew he was going to have to force himself to go out and socialize so this would be stepping way out of his comfort zone.

Mark made it a goal to say "Hi" to at least one woman a day for the first week, and if he did that he would reward himself by playing his favorite online video game, "World of Warcraft". If he did not complete his goal for each of the four weeks, he would donate $500 to charity at the end of that week.

For week two, he made it his goal to say, "Hi, how are you," and have at least a one-minute conversation with a woman once a day. If he did it, then he would reward himself by camping near Lake Tahoe for two nights with his best friend.

For week three, his goal was to say "Hi. How are you?" to at least one woman each day and then talk for a few minutes, doing his best to feel a connection. If he did it then he would reward himself with an ice cream and movie night with his friends.

For week four, his goal was to say "Hi, how are you" to at least one woman each day, ask her for her phone number, call her the next day to strengthen the connection, and then ask her out. If he did it, then he'd reward himself by attending a "Medieval Times" show with his date.

Mark didn't get to go camping, he instead donated $500 to Leukemia Lymphoma Society because he didn't complete week two. However, he followed through with the rest of the weeks and went on three dates to learn more about the women and to see what qualities he liked for a potential long-term partner.

A study in the journal *Psychological Science*, states that not only do we become more social and friendly people by enjoying what we are doing now, with whom we are interacting now, but we also tend to become more compassionate through the process of mindfulness. It lowers the stress in our thoughts and we become more outgoing and jovial people.

Believe that you will be where you want to be, and that you can do it if you put your mind to it, set goals, and have someone hold you accountable. Take your time to dream vividly about your dream. Of course, you are the person who is going to live your dream one day so you are the one who needs to put in the time and energy to dream it. You have to visualize the benefit of your achieved dream so clearly, so intensely, and so frequently that it will become a reality in your head before it becomes a reality on earth. It is this faith that will enable you to live your life one step at a time and enjoy that step with full presence of mind, or mindfulness.

SECRETS **to potential barriers**

Happiness

What if you were to believe that the universe is always plotting to do good for you even in the worst situation? Well, that is what one of the most significant leaders of the positive thinking movement, W. Clement Stone believed. He saw every challenge or difficult situation as something to empower and enrich himself. Imagine how your life might be different if you were to take in every moment from this perspective.

One of the many advantages of this type of thinking is that you will attract like-minded people and more of the perceived good things you desire. You can live happily in the present moment irrespective of the situation, the difficulties you are facing, or the amount of stress and workload that has been put on your shoulders. Imagine how much easier it would be to succeed and to be happy in life if you were expecting the universe to be on your side instead of against you.

Similar to the "everything happens for a reason" mindset, take the approach that whatever thing or person shows up in your life, there is a valid reason for it. There is something good for you in every situation of life. Whenever you feel that something is not going your way, or that something seemingly bad is happening, make a habit of asking yourself: "What valuable thing can I extract from this event?" and you will see and feel the transformations in your life.

You may be thinking that it is not easy to immediately change from a negative mindset to a positive one. However, the first step is to start thinking like an optimist. Imagine that the world is designed to work for you – not against you, and take a few seconds to really *feel* that the world is for you, truly believing it from your core. Since it takes approximately 30 days for a habit to be formed, it's important to take small action steps each day. For every negative thought you have, think of the inverse. For example, if you think, "Today is horrible and nothing is going my way", replace it with "Today is great. I am alive and breathing" or "Today is good. I have a job that provides me money to enjoy life and support my family (or anything that you feel grateful for that day)."

When you're first starting it, it is natural to keep some amount of negativity in dealing with your daily life situations. However, make it a daily habit and use constant reminders to improve the frequency of your positive attitude towards problems. It will take time, but this patience will bring you the life you've been waiting for.

VISUALIZATION AND SERENDIPITY

Serendipity is defined as "the occurrence and development of events by chance in a happy or beneficial way". You cannot predict the future, however you can strengthen your future and increase your chances of serendipitous experiences occurring when you take the time to visualize or meditate on exactly what you want. If we can spend some quiet time to reflect on our lives, we can begin to see how life has used serendipity to bring certain people, places and events in our lives.

During my first trip to Hawaii, I somehow managed to leave my raincoat in a friend's car on the way to the airport. I began to feel upset knowing it was a sunny and tropical place, and I didn't want to spend extra money from my limited budget on a raincoat. I took a few minutes to stop and visualize what I wanted in the future. Doing so, I closed my eyes, imagined myself stepping onto the plane, sitting next to a person who I would have a good conversation with, and offer a raincoat to me. I chuckled at the thought of this because I thought of how incredible it would be if that actually happened. Serendipitously, I met a man on the plane who had a raincoat in his bag that he didn't need,

Happiness

and graciously gave it to me. Leaving the airplane, I felt tears coming to my face and understood the power of visualization.

Use the power of your mind to dream, boldly believe that good things will come to you, and that they will in front of you each day. Maybe you are looking for a job, and a stranger you happen to talk to in the coffee shop happens to offer you a job. Sometimes it is as simple as taking the time to open your eyes and see things more clearly, or to take a look at things from new perspectives, possibly redefining your "why" for the way things happened. You will notice many happy and unexpected experiences come into your life that will bring you closer to your goal, whether it be making more money, finding an amazing romantic partner, getting into an impressive grad school, or overcoming a physical disability.

As a teenager, I struggled for years with back spasms, which were a result of the scoliosis (a curvature in the spine) I had. The harsh reality was that I would be standing talking to someone and anytime I'd feel anxious about something we were talking about, my back would go into spasm. Besides being embarrassed, it was painful and I wanted more than anything to be "normal" and pain free. Doctors prescribed sedatives in the hopes that it would stop the spasms. Physical therapists introduced me to specific back exercises hoping to reduce the spasms. Neither worked. I had lost hope.

Because of the constant spasms, I thought my lower back muscles were being overworked. If only my back could take a break and simply relax! That was it! I needed to get myself to relax my muscles by being in the present moment. I tested it out. I closed my eyes and repeated the word "relax" as I began to sink more and more into the present moment. I could feel my spasms begin to recede, until they stopped for a few seconds.

I was on to something. I knew that my spasms got worse when I felt anxious in social situations. Therefore, I would imagine being in those uncomfortable situations and I would repeat the word "relax" until my spasms stopped. I would get into the present so much I could imagine the specific muscles in my back moving. Every day for the next four weeks, I repeated the word "relax" whenever I felt uncomfortable and miraculously my back spasms completely disappeared. It has been 13 years, and those spasms have not come back.

This unexpected discovery of the ability to use the present moment to relax was incredible. It completely changed my life. If you are struggling with any type of physical disability or pain that medical professionals told you was incurable, take a second to focus on the present moment. Allow your energy to focus toward the specific place in your body where the pain is. Now get into a relaxed state of mind by repeating the word "relax" so that it is the only thought in your head, allowing your body and mind to be completely present.

The possibilities of *present moment* are endless, especially when combined with visualization and firmly believing that serendipitous experiences will occur in your life.

What serendipitous things happened to you today?

Spend tomorrow completely in the present moment, leaving behind any negative thoughts about yesterday, or any anxious feelings about your future. If these thoughts begin to sprout, take a second to get out of your head by telling your mind to relax and focus on your body and your breathing, so that you can slide back into the present moment. In addition, keep track on your smart phone (or a piece of paper in your pocket) of how it feels to be *in the present moment* state of mind. If you enjoyed it, I urge you to try it again.

16

Scientific Studies Showing The Positive Effects Of Living In The Present Moment

Science supports both mindfulness and mindful-meditation. Mindfulness is defined as "a mental state achieved by focusing one's awareness on the present moment, while calmly acknowledging and accepting one's feelings, thoughts, and bodily sensations, used as a therapeutic technique." Mindful Meditation is a form of meditation that focuses primarily on breathing and positive attitudes. Its purpose is to acquire a healthy and balanced state of mind. It has been shown to inhibit relaxation, reduce anxiety, and encourage positive thought patterns, such as an increased love, kindness, and compassion toward yourself and others.

The *Journal of Health Psychology* and showed that mindfulness not only makes you feel mentally less stressed, but it also decreases the levels of the stress hormone "cortisol".

Donna was a woman who had a near death experience. As she was rolled into the hospital on the stretcher she was suffering from severe jaundice, making her feel exhausted and so weak she nearly collapsed. Doctors rushed her in the ICU telling her that she had liver failure from poisoning. Her liver enzyme levels were over 7000, with normal levels being about 1. After pumping 70 pounds of fluids into her body, the physicians told her that the only way she would survive would be with a liver transplant. However, being a firm believer of holistic practices, she refused the transplant liver offer. She insisted that she would heal herself by focusing on positive thinking, eating well, being very present to what is going on in her body, and overall "loving" her liver.

Donna went internal and believed she could heal from the inside out and became hyperaware of her liver. She had a lot of love for it. She would talk to it and be totally with it. She repeated this process for five days, and miraculously she was back to normal levels at the end of that period. She surrounded herself with positive people, and pushed away all negativity, because it was poison. She directed her love to the present moment, right here and now, not letting the worst of her fears enter her mind.

In 2013, researchers from the University of California compared the efficiency of two groups of college students. The first group was asked to take mindfulness classes for two weeks where they were taught how to use mindfulness in every situation. They were trained on how to stay focused on the present moment without being distracted. The other group went to a nutrition class where they learned about strategies of healthy eating during which they were asked to keep a food log.

The first group of students experienced improvements in their working memory and also performed better on the verbal reasoning section of the GRE (a test administered for graduate school applicants). Thus, these researchers advocate the use of living in the present moment for improving one's cognitive function.

Jason had difficulty listening and trouble remembering things that were said to him just minutes before. His partner would often get frustrated and impatient with him because of this. For instance, his partner would ask him to do a task and minutes later he would completely forget the task. He hated it because he didn't want to forget, it was just hard for him to focus.

Jason was determined to improve this part of himself. He tried memory games such as Luminosity, which slightly improved his memory. Then he discovered mindfulness. He learned that if he completely focused on the person talking to him, ignoring all the external distractions by putting an imaginary brick wall up so that he could focus on the one person who was talking to him, he could remember what was said. He'd completely listen to the words, and how they were being said. As the words were being said he would focus on the feeling the words would create inside his body. The interesting thing was that he learned that by feeling emotions in the present moment, he could recall things much easier. However, if he just listened to the words, he would easily forget what was said because no emotions were created. In addition, he'd write the assignment on a small notepad that he kept in his back pocket to ensure that he'd remember what his partner had asked him to do.

When we focus on the present moment, a new door opens, as we perceive life differently. Instead of feeling regret from past mistakes or worries for the future, we can surpass the trap of these undesired emotions by getting completely present. If your mind begins to get stuck in a state of fear or guilt, you can shift your thoughts with mindful-meditation.

MINDFUL-MEDITATION

Here are the steps to mindfully meditate:

1. Sit in a quiet area and focus on your breathing, allowing thoughts to enter and exit your mind without judgment, with your primary focus on your breathing.

2. If your body feels sensations such as a tingle or an itch, let them pass without judgment. Be aware of your body from head to toe.

3. Take in all the senses including touch, sight, smell, sound, and taste, allowing them to flow in and out of your mind without judgment.

4. Let all emotions enter your mind and be present. Name each one of them without passing judgment. For example, "anger", "fear", "joy", "sadness", or "disgust". Then let them go.

There was a study in the journal called *Psychological Science*, which showed that "being mindful can help us objectively analyze ourselves for amplifying or diminishing our own flaws far beyond reality."

Susan had finally found the man of her dreams. He was intelligent, athletic, fun, and free-spirited. However, sometimes during conversation, she would feel disconnected, as if he simply did not understand what she was saying to him. This would cause outbursts of anger and frustration because she could not understand why he wasn't feeling the same way as her. For instance, she would passionately tell him about an organic food delivery business she wanted to start and how it could revolutionize the entire food system, and he didn't seem to understand the importance of it. She longed for deep understanding and connection with her boyfriend.

Susan decided to be mindful. She took this frustration and chose to look at it from an outside perspective. She thought to herself, if I were to place myself on top of a mountain and look down at the situation with my boyfriend, what would it look like? She laughed and sighed, thinking that she simply didn't understand him. He isn't the same person as her, so of course the way he responds to things will be completely different than the way she would respond.

Susan decided to not focus on what was "wrong with him", and instead worked on herself to improve her social skills in order to understand why she reacted the way she did. She learned that it is impossible to change people, and that the only person she had control over was herself. She discovered the power of curiosity, and how to ask strong open-ended questions so that she could understand her husband's way of thinking. Within a few weeks, this prolonged confusion had come to a peaceful understanding of each others' beliefs.

In 2011, there was a research study conducted into the help of mindfulness in patients with arthritis for handling stress. The results of this study were published the same year in the journal called *Annals of Rheumatic Disease*. The researchers proved the positive effect of mindfulness training for lowering the stress and fatigue of rheumatoid arthritis patients.

Greg was a middle-aged man who suffered from arthritis most of his life. Much of the arthritis flare-ups were a result of being stressed. He had a tendency to be in his head most of the day and feeling anxious about new situations. For example, he loved getting to know strangers even though he would stress out about initiating conversations with them because of his fear of rejection.

Greg took a leap and tested out life in the present moment. He took the initiative to put his energy and focus on his body to be more present with himself. When he felt like he was getting too much in his head, he would hit the reset button by taking a few deep breaths, and ask himself "Where are you now?" Then he'd confidently initiate conversation with strangers. Being present gave him peace of mind, and he noticed his flare-ups were less common and significantly reduced.

When you live in the present moment, you become more aware of the things that are happening within you and immediately around you. This phenomenon of living in the moment helps your brain to have better control over processing pain and emotions, and then moving forward with your life. If you resist feeling the pain you experience, you are not allowing your mind and body to grasp reality. You are preventing yourself from letting go by running away from the pain of the past.

After my father passed, I felt nothing but anger toward him. He got sick and overdosed on drugs. Even though I was upset, I had

Happiness

already accepted the fact that some people can't control the fact that they have an addictive personality and therefore can't stop, due to a chemical dependence in the brain.

I had a choice to remain angry at the situation or I could focus my energy on the happy times we had together. In that moment, I grabbed a piece of paper and wrote down all the positive memories I wanted to cherish. Some of them were the time we spent a day people-watching in San Francisco, the nights we'd use the telescope to check out the moon and stars, as well as the times we'd challenge each other to talk to strangers to see if we'd get into a captivating conversation. I came up with 100 memories and told myself that I would put it away for one-week, and in the meantime embrace my emotions. Then when one-week was up, my reward would be to read and replay the memories in my mind.

In order to embrace my emotions I needed to be completely present with how I was feeling in each moment of the day. The heart-wrenching pain from losing my father mixed with the thousands of tears that reluctantly needed to be shed, as well as the anger surrounding the question "Why?" all needed to be felt. Whenever I was feeling extreme emotions, almost to the point I couldn't take anymore, I'd take out my journal and write. I'd write until my mind was clear.

Even though I wanted more than anything to ignore and hide those painful emotions, I knew deep down that feeling them was the only way to move forward. Otherwise those painful feelings would persist, and continue to creep up. As weeks went on, I felt better and completely accepted what had happened. The thoughts surrounding my father's life and the times we shared together will forever be cherished.

Scientists at the University of Oregon found that those who practice integrative body-mind training resulted in some changes in the brain's signaling and connections. These changes were seen to be protective against mental illness. Therefore, living in the present moment can actually improve the quality of the brain tissue you possess.

As per a study in *Perspectives on Psychological Science*, the habit of being mindful every time helps us to develop four elements that boost our mental (and thus, physical) health. These elements include awareness of body, awareness of self, regulation of attention, and regulation of emotion.

Jason was flying high in the sky from San Francisco to New York. The man sitting next to him had a young child who kept screaming loudly seemingly whenever Jason shut his eyes to take a rest. He could feel his body heating up as his anger and frustration levels began to rise. All he longed for was to get a bit of shuteye. He wanted to say something to the parent but he didn't want to create any awkward energy with his seat neighbor, considering he'd be sitting next to him for the next four hours. He chose to be fully present by focusing on each of his breaths. He would imagine each of his breaths as a color depending on how he was feeling. Blue when he was feeling peaceful and red when angry. He looked at the experience as a game and embraced the sounds to the point where he actually enjoyed them.

A study conducted at the University of Utah found that the people trained in living in the present moment not only claimed better control of their emotions and moods, but that it also helped them to sleep better. There was lower activation of their brains at bedtime, which benefited their sleep quality and ability to manage stress.

Samantha went for months with very little sleep after splitting up with her husband. It would often take her hours to fall asleep, and as time passed she got more frustrated. She tried reading, watching T.V., and talking to friends on the phone – nothing worked. Once she fell asleep, she would usually wake at least two or three times, and struggle to fall asleep again. She refused to take sleeping medications because of the harmful side effects. People at work began making negative comments about her appearance. She noticed herself drowsing off from time to time and she had challenges staying focused at work. She knew things would continue to get worse if she didn't change something.

Lying in bed with tears flowing down her face, she remembered once hearing, "Your body has so much wisdom. Go deep inside and listen to it." She never fully understood what it meant until that moment. She lay as still as possible, as if she were a manikin, and she felt a sense of relief. She felt her stomach slowly rise and descend as she lay there quietly, replacing her stressful thoughts of her work and failed relationship with that of calming peace. It flowed throughout her body, and she fell fast asleep.

CHOOSING THE PAST, Present, or Future

What if your past was completely wiped away? Everything has been erased including the enjoyable and unpleasant memories. All your new memories in the present moment are immediately forgotten because they have become your past. For example, you may be having the most intriguing conversation of your life, but it is impossible to remember what you just said because your past does not exist. It is impossible to remember anything. What would your world look like if the past did not exist?

What if your future were to completely disappear? All you have is your past and you only mentally and physically function in the present moment, with no direction. Planning things does not exist in this non-future world. It is impossible to create dreams or goals. The door to your future is nailed shut, leaving you in total darkness. What if this was the world in which you lived?

What if your present moments were wiped away? Only your past and your future exist. You body has become frozen and unable to move because your body is the only thing that is eternally present. Therefore, your past is stuck. It is dead. No new memories can be created because there is no present moment. On the other hand, if your future existed without present moments, then it would be frozen as well and your life would have already been planned.

Instead, your future is there to be guided by your present moment because your present moment is clay-like and can be formed into a beautiful sculpture of past experiences and future dreams. Therefore, the present moment has a direct link to the past and the future. The future is guided by the present. Hence, the present moment needs to be fully embraced because it molds your past and designs your future.

We were given the ability to choose to be dreamy and live in the future, or be present and enjoy each task at hand. We can live in the past and reminisce on either beautiful or terrible memories. Although, once again it is only the present moment that positively or negatively affects everything in your life – every feeling you get, everything you learn, everything you experience. As you can see, each of the three time periods are important and must be used in synchronicity. However, the leader is the present moment, in which the formula for happiness was created. That being a mindset of 10% living in the past to learn from your mistakes and triumphs, 10% living in the future to create goals, and 80% living in the present moment to enjoy and fully absorb each moment on earth.

Which world do you choose to live in - the past, the present, or the future?

The next time you have three hours free, use them to test the following out for yourself. Take one of the hours and use it to live completely in the past. At the end of the hour, take note of how it felt.

Now for the second hour, live only in the present. Just do stuff. Don't think about what you're going to do, just do it. How does that feel?

Now use the third hour to live only in the future. Imagine your life in the future. Let your dreams and fear roam free. How did that hour feel?

Now ask yourself to choose your favorite time period and vow to spend a good amount of your life in it. For example, you can spend 80% in the present and divide the other 20% between the past and future.

17

Great Minds Think In The Present Moment

The Nobel Peace Prize winner and one of the most beautiful people to ever walk the earth, Mother Teresa, believed that each moment is all we need to be happy. Being happy about what we have now and what we have created (both good and bad) is one of the most rewarding feelings we can experience. You can use this moment to make the choice to either continue living on the road you've been living, or change gears by shifting what you focus on. Are your thoughts focused on the past, present or the future?

Sarah was focused on the qualities she didn't have, and the negative qualities that she did have because she'd constantly compare himself to others. She viewed herself as not good looking enough to have a boyfriend, mostly because she didn't like her long nose and she thought she was too tall at six-feet. These self-defeating thoughts prevented her from going out and living the life she desired.

Little did she know that many men are attracted to women of all shapes and sizes. The limiting thoughts would enter her head every time she went out with friends to social events. When men talked to her, she always thought that they just wanted to sleep with her or that they had found out that she made good money working as an accountant at a top financial firm. She wanted to do anything to get these thoughts out of her head.

Sarah learned of the present moment, and how much more enjoyable it is to live in. Her strategy was to enter each social situation taking on the character traits of someone she admired, Brene Brown, who inspired her with a "Vulnerability" video that she watched on YouTube. She imagined Brene Brown, who emphasizes "Fake it 'til you become it," saying to her, "Just be yourself by being open and vulnerable. Everyone has insecurities so instead of letting them hold you back, embrace them and let your favorite qualities about yourself shine."

From this point on, these words of wisdom that she created completely removed fear from her mind, as she was able to look at every situation from a non-judgmental one, embracing her favorite qualities about herself, which were her beautiful eyes and long brown hair, not to mention her gregarious personality that brought smiles to people's faces as she entered a room. One month later, she had a boyfriend who absolutely adores her.

Who do you admire or look up to? Where in your life can you use this person to get rid of fear of the future to get you to enjoy the present moment?

I had a three months before graduate school and I wanted to spend it with my father since I knew I'd be super busy for the next few years. I knew his health and financial situation were declining and I wanted to help him out as much as I could. I chose to move in with him for those months before grad school to keep him company and help him get a small consulting business started.

We'd spend many hours working the business, getting most of our clients from Craigslist. It was difficult and we hardly made enough money to afford enough food and a cheap place to stay for the night. Sometimes when we couldn't find a place, we'd spend the night in my car to stay warm. It was hard to stay optimistic, and I didn't want my dad to be homeless when I was in grad school. Therefore, we worked as hard as we could to get his business off of the ground.

I got a taste of what it felt like to be homeless, as we were spending some nights in my car. My heart grew bigger for people who are struggling with their finances, as well as homeless people who had hit rock bottom. Over these few months, I talked to many people who were homeless and living on the streets. Some of them were addicted to drugs. Some had psychological issues, such as schizophrenia. Others got laid off from work, and didn't have family to fall back on. Each one of them had feelings of love and a heart for helping others, as well as the skill to feel grateful to be alive.

A few years after I had become a life coach, I felt it was my duty to introduce these people to the power of the present moment, and how it transformed my life, as well as hundreds of people I'd worked with. It was my mission to go on the streets of San Francisco for two hours every Saturday, aiming to wash away all fear and judgment by being in the present moment, and communicate with each person who looked homeless. I wanted to give them hope and inspire them. I asked each of them to name three things they felt grateful for.

The most common answers were "I'm grateful for being alive", "I'm grateful for the sunshine", "I'm grateful for living in this beautiful city", "I'm grateful for meeting you." This often brought smiles to their faces.

Then the conversation would shift to ones of goals and dreams for the future – some being "to create a successful foster care home", "to bring peace in our community", and "to be a successful guitarist in a band". It was amazing to see and feel them dream, despite hitting rock bottom, and not giving up on life.

Lastly, I would leave with a request for each of them. I requested that every day each person I talked to think and feel grateful for at least three things, and to state the gratitudes out loud. In addition, I gave each of them a bracelet with the words "Where are you now?" to use as a reminder to remain in the present moment, because many of their thoughts were centered on their pain from the past.

THE POETS

Enjoying the nature around us, feeling the feelings of the present moment, and hearing the music hidden in the silence were some of the chief topics from the most profound poets who ever lived. According to William Wordsworth, life is divided into three terms – that which was, which is, and which will be. He advised us to learn from the past to profit by the present, and from the present to live better in the future. Thus, life according to him is a learning process. He emphasized that while learning and experiencing life, to make sure to enjoy each and every breath you take.

Poets and artists see the world differently: they are filled with creative wonder and curiosity. Another great poet who pleaded for living in the present and making the most of it was Ralph Waldo Emerson. Emerson once claimed that humans are always getting ready to live but never actually live. He separated himself from anything except the present moment by claiming that he had nothing to do with his past, nor with his future. He pleaded to finish each day and to be done with it. Then he'd start tomorrow as a new day to be begun serenely and with too high a spirit to be encumbered with old nonsense.

THE AUTHORS

Henry David Thoreau believed that we must live in the present and thus launch ourselves on every wave. This way, we will find our eternity in each and every moment. He said that the fools are people who stand on their island of opportunities and keep looking toward another land. In fact, there is no other land or life on earth but this – the one that we are living in this moment.

The greatest teachers of all times who taught about life also advocated living in the present moment. According to Louise L. Hay, the author of "Heal Your Life", the point of power is always in the present moment. Deepak Chopra, one of the best-selling authors of the self-help books of modern times, says that life gives you plenty of time to do whatever you want to do if you stay in the present moment.

Dale Carnegie, the best-selling author of the book "How to Win Friends and Influence People", said that the only life we are sure of is "today", thus, we should make the most of it. He once said "We are all dreaming of some magical rose garden over the horizon — instead of enjoying the roses that are blooming outside our windows today."

Many people think that the primary cause of their unhappiness is the situation they are in. However, this thought is contradicted by the fact that many others would feel happy in the same situation they are in now. Suppose you get panicked on a roller coaster, thinking that you might lose your consciousness while riding it. There is always another person sitting on the same roller coaster who gets an incredible adrenaline rush and an immense feeling of happiness by riding it. So, the situations are not the root cause of all evil, but it is our perception of the moment we live in that determines whether we enjoy those moments or not.

Eckhart Tolle, the author of "The Power of NOW", believes that it is never the situation but your thoughts that lead to your happiness or unhappiness. He further claims that life is not yesterday or tomorrow, but it is right here, right now.

Leo Tolstoy, the author of the highly acclaimed novel "War and Peace", was so amused by the passion of living in the present moment that he requested that the people to have that passion, by exclaiming: "Remember that there is only one important time and it is Now. The present moment is the only time over which we have dominion. The most important person is always the person with whom you are, who is right before you, for who knows if you will have dealings with any other person in the future? The most important pursuit is making that person, the one standing at you side, happy, for that alone is the pursuit of life."

OTHER SIGNIFICANT FIGURES

Albert Einstein, one of the greatest and well-recognized minds of all time believed that most people live their lives preparing for the future and that the best way to live is to live as if there were no future.

Abraham Lincoln, the 16th President of the U.S., mentioned that the best thing about our future is that it doesn't come at once. In fact, it comes only one day at a time. So, make the most of every moment you live, as it is the real secret to happiness and success.

These successful people who walked the earth left us some of the most important lessons from their lives, which are worth understanding to achieve our highest potential. One such lesson is the ability to direct our thoughts and focus on the present moment, where you are now, and what your body is saying, based on the position of your hands or legs. It is not the past that they kept living in. It was not the fear of the future, but instead the present moment that they lived, breathed, and soared in.

These brilliant individuals understood that they could

only move ahead of their past mistakes and achieve what they desired by making most of the present moment. They thought cautiously and then made decisions swiftly. Then, carrying the weapon of self-discipline on their shoulders, they executed the decisions they'd chosen to make. All along this process of execution, they enjoyed each and every moment with faith and determination in their hearts that their decision would be carried out successfully.

Living in the present moment may seem simple, however, many of us doubt our own abilities and find this process very difficult, during which we start losing the power of self-discipline – even to the point that we don't have the discipline to commit to living in the present moment.

Sean loved to make people laugh hysterically, to the point where they'd be rolling out of their seats and feel like they'd just completed a major abdominal workout. However, the thought of being up on stage and performing brought instant fear to his body and mind. For three years, fear and nerves blocked him from getting on stage. He imagined people making fun of him, or forgetting what to say, or even falling on stage. These self-defeating thoughts pushed away his dream, as he got busier with other things in life, other than his true passion of entertaining people.

One day, Sean finally gained the courage to just do it. He got out of his head where his self-defeating saboteurs lived, and became keenly aware of the present moment – things other than the conversations in his head. Every morning he would spend 30 minutes meditating to become very present, letting thoughts flow in and out of his head, listening to the beautiful sounds of life around him, including birds, cars, voices in the distance, and his breathing.

Sean used this ability to feel an overwhelming sense of peace in the present moment and combined it with the power of visualization. He would imagine himself driving to the venue, entering the room full of people smiling and observing him stepping onto the stage, then grabbing the mic. He then saw himself performing comedic acts and looking around at a fully engaged crowd, giving him a roaring applause as he was stepping down from the stage.

After conquering all the internal battles using visualization and present moment awareness, Sean finally took to the stage to perform and the roaring crowd absolutely loved him. He had an unforgettably euphoric experience, a feeling he'd never felt before.

18

The Puzzle of The Present Moment

You have 24 hours a day and seven days a week. You have a choice of how you allocate your time each day for every activity. You're also able to simultaneously ignore the troubling moments of your past and choose to not focus on the unpredictable and uncontrollable future.

You have the choice to use your time wisely by being aware of the things that complete the puzzle of life – things that stem from being conscious of the present. You know that you are in the present and that's all you need to know to move on from the past and be excited for the future. As introduced in the first section, everyone's trying to complete his or her own life puzzle. The challenge is figuring out what pieces actually fit into *your* life puzzle.

THE CHANGE

You change every day. Physiologically speaking, all the cells in your body change constantly and in just seven years, you're no longer the same person on a molecular or cellular level. Your body moves forward from the past and once you reach 70, you'll have changed 10 times. If your physical body can move forward, then surely your mind and heart can do the same.

Even if we are the ones inhabiting our bodies, it doesn't automatically mean that we already know every single detail about ourselves. You may not have memorized every single organ or part of your body, but the idea being proposed here is that people are only at the tip of the iceberg when it comes to being familiar with *whom* they actually are. This leaves much room for discovery and the other pieces of your identity can be found in your subconscious.

There are times when the subconscious lets out bits of information that we have stored in our mind; things that may help us become more familiar with who we are and what we dream to be. The mind is often considered an untapped well of memories and information; and yet in this chaotic world, it is not always easy to find time to explore your mind extensively, although it is imperative for accessing answers. This is one of the reasons that it's important to set time aside for "quiet-time" or meditation, to allow you to connect with who you are becoming, and what you want in this life.

As you discover more about yourself, you'll be able to see things from a new perspective, because you are slowly becoming more familiar with who you are, how you think, and how you interpret various situations. You are slowly transforming into a person who can contribute much more to yourself and to the people you love.

Further, since you are now aware of what your past has developed or created in you, you can learn and take the opportunity to grow from your painful experiences and cease resenting them.

. . .

MOMENTS TO BE Present
1. Conversation

When participating in a conversation, being fully present with your mind and body are imperative. You will notice how your listening skills greatly increase in the present moment, which will allow you to have long, engaging conversations. Also, it is much easier to create curious questions while having a conversation in the present, not allowing thoughts of what you should say next, to enter your mind. For more information about engaging in incredible conversation with anyone, take a look at my book called The Conversation Method.

Meeting new people is also a great way to live in the present. There will always be space for new people in your life, so don't limit yourself to just a couple of friends or a few relatives. If you're not much of an extrovert, you can try and be friends with your co-workers, neighbors, or classmates. You can even go to events you enjoy by searching on www.meetup.com. New relationships open new doors in your life and these opportunities help you have a more

wonderful present.

2. Hobbies

Hobbies are activities in which you can fully immerse yourself in the moment. Find hobbies that are fun and practice keeping yourself in the present moment. Many people who seek out hobbies such as rock climbing or yoga are more prone to being in the present, as it is necessary to be aware of what the body and mind are doing while climbing or holding a position.

Art offers various avenues for those who want to explore their artistic expression. You can sketch, paint, and sculpt anything you can conceive and through your creations, you'll also see the extent of your current abilities and what you can still work on to improve your talents. Art is limitless and it's a great way to use the present moment to explore your thoughts, beliefs, feelings, and desires. Further, people can see the depth and beauty of your life through your art.

3. Music

Listen to music that can help soothe your mind and aid you as you discover more of yourself. With numerous genres available, you'll surely find something that can create an ambience conducive to meditation.

Many prefer to listen to music without words, such as classical music like Mozart, or ambient nature sounds as they meditate daily. Listening to Mozart, Pachelbel, Beethoven, Tchaikovsky, and many other renowned classical composers, has a tendency to simplify the process of self-discovery and make your time in the present more productive.

4. Working Out

It is easy to get distracted by other people working out in the gym that you lose focus on your workout. While working out, focus on your breathing. Become fully present and be aware of your body movements. Imagine how your muscles, joints, and bones are working synergistically so that you can move, and how they are aligned in relation to one another.

5. Spend More Time with Your Loved Ones

Maybe you've heard the saying that "Love is spelled T-I-M-E." This short, yet meaningful statement is a condensed message of children to their parents, of parents to their adult children, and of people to their friends.

As Steve Jobs put it, "My favorite things in life don't cost any money. It's really clear that the most precious resource we all have is time." Sadly, not many recognize this because people are too busy planning. The greatest gift you can give yourself is to *choose* to be happy – right now, right this second, in the present moment.

Your loved ones deserve and need your time, whether they know and say it or not. What better way to spend the present than with your beloved family and friends? After all, no one on their deathbed has ever said that they should've invested more time in their work than in their family. Money and a successful career can't hug you back and neither can they wipe your tears away or listen to your problems. Spend time with the ones you love and your present will be well lived.

Visiting a relative you haven't seen for many years also allows you to extend love and care to other people. You'll be given the chance to share what you have learned from your past and how you are now looking at your future.

Your knowledge will help considerably more people find their way in life and how they can fully live in the present too. You know how difficult it can be to go through painful experiences and be afraid of an unknown future, so the experience you once shunned is now also part of your inspiring testimony to others. You've now become a light in their darkness.

COMPLETING the Puzzle of Time

Time is the most precious gift that you are given. You

are given a choice for how you start and end each day, just as it is up to you to decide how to spend each of the priceless seconds, minutes, and hours you are given. It is up to you to make the most out of each day because you never know when the doors to your life will be permanently shut.

Being only 10 years of age and newly conscious after months of rehabilitation in the Children's Hospital in Detroit, I felt as if my world had fallen apart. My grandmother told me that I was in a plane crash and in a coma for a month. Minutes later she grabbed my hand and sat on the hospital bed next to me to give me the worst news of all. She told me that my mom didn't survive the crash. At that moment I felt completely helpless and I knew my world would never be the same.

For years I felt confused as to why my mom had to die. She was such a good person who genuinely wanted the best for everyone. I remember times when she would insist on taking gifts to children on Christmas, and to less fortunate families on Thanksgiving. I remember how she would say prayers with me and have me name things I was grateful for every day before I went to sleep. I remember those moments when my mom would spot a monarch butterfly, she'd point out how magnificent it looked, with its beautifully designed orange and black wings. Even though I cherished each of these precious memories, there was this burning anger deep inside surrounding the question, "Why did this have to happen to me?"

One day as I was sitting on a park bench, I began to think of times when I talked back to my mother and it would make her so angry. Feelings of regret flowed throughout my body and I felt I didn't do enough for her while she was still alive. I took a deep breath and all of a sudden I spotted a magnificent monarch butterfly, gracefully landing on my shoulder. I felt as if my mom was trying to tell me something -- that life has many precious moments and if I continued to live with feelings of worry and regret from the past, I would miss out on the true essence of life, which exists only in the present moment. If I hadn't been fully present, I may have never noticed the butterfly or feel the message my mom was trying to tell me. In one minute, life could be swept right from under my feet, just as my mom's life had been taken so abruptly with her decision to board the plane. I felt peaceful knowing that all I needed was right here, right now, in the present moment. I was finally able to let go of the past and move on.

The past, present, and future are all that ever exist. Experiences and memories accumulate from your past and are continuously gained in the present, while you're creating your new future. Future goals affect your decisions in the present because of your personal desires.

How you manage these elements define who you are. You're either living in the past, present, or future – you *can't* exist in these three time periods at the same time.

Completing the puzzle of life demands a deeper awareness of your identity and a consistent desire to know where you are in the timeline. You can't complete the puzzle if you don't acknowledge the importance of the most significant piece of the puzzle: the present. To know where you are and where your energy is flowing is just the beginning to existing in the present.

Take a look at yourself in this moment and think about where you are in life right now. Think about who you have become. Are you using your present moments to follow your passions? Do your actions, thoughts, and words remain consistent with your desire to live the life of your dreams? If not, what do you need to remove from your life to get where you want to be?

Many are just partly enjoying the gift of the present. Some are able to become fully aware of the present, and others take a relatively long time to get to that state. No matter what your pace is, though, having the knowledge that the present moment exists, and taking steps to become more aware of your mind and body will lead you to a happy, enjoyable life.

ACCEPT what you can't change and be thankful for what you can

Some things are unchangeable, uncontrollable, and unforeseeable, but these things keep life interesting. Instead of dodging something that can't be changed, embrace the unchangeable with your changeable heart. Take a deep breath, and fully commit to being present. Now that you've let all the past go, and allowed the future to be what it is, relax your shoulders as you feel the weight lifted.

You can't control how people will perceive a situation. However, you can change the way you look at the situation. Learn and grow from it. You'll feel pain and you'll get disappointed every now and then because life isn't perfect, as the people in it are nowhere near to perfection. Be thankful that you're alive, breathing, and have the opportunity to embrace a new life in the present moment.

19

Q & A

11. Q & A From Students About Letting Go Of The Past, Not Worrying About The Future, and Living In The Present Moment

In this last section, I asked hundreds of students, readers, and colleagues if they had any burning questions about letting go of the past, not worrying about the future, and living in the present moment. I hope the answers to these questions will continue to point you in the right direction so that you can continue live a life of peace and joy in the present moment. The strategies discussed below are ones that have worked for hundreds of my students, as well as myself.

HOW DO I not let others affect my focus?

The easiest way would be to stick some headphones in your ears and listen to music. However, assuming that you don't have headphones and you want to train your subconscious mind to be more present you can use meditative strategies.

To start out, I recommend beginning with meditating for 15 minutes twice a day (morning and night). While sitting quietly in a place of solitude, focus all your attention on your breathing to align yourself with your body. Let thoughts flow in and out of your head. Do not focus on one thought for long, simply let it enter and release it. If a thought persists for long, put all your attention on your breathing. Is it slow? Is it fast? What color is it? Can you give your breath a name?

This will train you to re-center yourself once you feel you are losing your focus on whatever task you are performing.

After a few days, increase your meditation time to 30 minutes twice a day (morning and night). You'll begin to see and feel a positive shift in your ability to sustain attention in the present moment. And when your focus begins to slip, you can always refocus your attention on your breathing.

HOW DO I avoid being upset by others?

Some emotions are controllable, while others aren't — both are okay. What is important is what you do with those emotions that upset you. What is the underlying reason for why you are upset? Take a second to think about it. Did he or she say something that struck a nerve? Talk to this person, expressing to him or her how their words and actions are affecting you, causing you to drift from enjoying your present moment. Otherwise, the person may never know that he or she is upsetting you and it will continue to eat you up inside.

You can use the Feel, Empathize, Question method. Here's how it works. First let the person know that you want to talk to him or her, and be sure you are in an area where you can give each other your full attention. Then begin your statement expressing how you feel. For example, "I feel upset when you agree to do the dishes and you don't do them." Then empathize with something like, "I understand that it can be hard to remember sometimes," and follow it with a question such as, "What can I do to help?"

HOW CAN I use the past to learn from, instead of dwelling on it?

The past is filled with many emotions, both happy and sad. Allow your thoughts to consist of 10% Past (to learn from), 10% Future (to dream), and 80% Present (to enjoy the moment).

The past is in the past for a reason. It is over. Dwelling on your past thoughts is like trapping yourself inside a prison cell because your past thoughts, words, and actions cannot escape. Although you can let go of negative memories of the past so that they feel like nothing more than a mere illusion, you cannot erase them because they were already brought into existence.

Spend a few minutes to take the energy that once was in those moments. Embrace those remaining feelings from the past, and ask, "What can I learn from this past moment? What is important about it? How can I use it to improve my present and future moments?" Then write the thoughts down, and use the power of your mind to let go of the past to keep it in prison, bury it, or throw it into the sea. Create a metaphor that resonates with you to keep from drifting back to the past. Then most importantly, move forward with your life so that you can develop new pasts from your present moments that lie in front of you.

. . .

HOW CAN I forgive myself from the past?

Use this moment to imagine the past event you have trouble forgiving yourself from. Now take long, full deep breaths, inhaling oxygen into your lungs so that your belly is fully expanded, and scream at the top of your lungs, "I forgive myself!" until you feel like shedding tears. Repeat this process until you feel complete.

Then spend the next minutes to feel grateful (I know it's hard) for the past because you can learn from it. Be grateful for the choices you have in front of you. Be grateful for the freedom you are given. Be grateful for understanding how you can use the present moment to design a new past and a new future. Continue this process for 30 days (or longer), to turn it into a positive habit.

HOW CAN I be proud of myself?

Step into your past and think of one accomplishment you have made in your lifetime. Start with the simple things. You learned how to walk. You learned to read. You learned to drive a car. You graduated high school (or perhaps college). You made friends with whom you can communicate with. You have the ability to design your future. You have the power to start new this very moment so be proud of yourself.

You are amazing. You are amazing. You are amazing. Yes, I repeated that three times and I would keep repeating it, but I won't. Okay once more – You are amazing! Look deep inside yourself. Give yourself permission to be proud of yourself. Think of something you accomplished today and feel grateful for it. Be proud.

Make it a habit, by using the next 30 days to write down at least one thing you're proud of during each day and let me know how you feel in 30 days. Email me at: matt@rootscoaching.com

HOW CAN I get over having too high of expectations for others, while not giving too much of myself to people who don't deserve it?

You can't control anyone's actions or how they will perform. You can only control your actions. Understand that he or she has a different way of thinking than you. They've had unique experiences throughout their lifetime that have formed them into the person they are today.

Find out what matters to them because what you see as important, they may not even think twice about. Are they doing their best? If not, ask them what they need from you to improve.

If this person doesn't "deserve" your high expectations, then how come you are keeping them on a pedestal? Learn to be accepting and be okay with what is in the present moment. Welcome, encourage, and support these people with love, especially if they are giving it all they've got.

HOW DO I stop letting what others think of me get in the way of being myself?

Who are you? No, really, *who* are you? Everyone has different sides to him or herself based on whom they are around. Are you being your true self or are you hiding a locked up version of you in the closet? What would happen if you let this person out, not regarding anyone else's expectations? I demand that you test it out for a day. Then another, and let me know how it goes. E-mail me at: matt@rootscoaching.com

. . .

Happiness

WHY IS LIVING in the present moment important?

The present moment is all there is. It forms your future and past. There are so many incredible moments when you look through the window of your past, and it can be freeing when looking at what is possible in the window to the future. All of your past and future moments are created now, in the present moment. When you are fully embracing the present moment, you will experience feelings of peace, absolute creativity, wisdom, and happiness.

HOW CAN I value each moment of my life without letting others steal that moment from me?

What if this person (who is stealing your moment) is desperate for attention? Instead of seeing this person as your enemy, what if you were to shift your perspective to seeing them as a child who needs your help. How would you treat them? When someone is "stealing" your moment, what if you were to join him or her and use the present moment to feel excited, happy, or any other positive emotion for the other person? Often times, once you match and embrace the other persons' presence instead of getting angry and frustrated that they are "stealing your moment", he or she will become more accepting by letting you have your moment.

HOW CAN I make the moments I have stay focused on the positive without going to the negative?

Negativity comes from the thoughts bouncing around in your head. Once you grab onto a negative thought and squeeze it, nasty yellowish-green negative energy juice will flow into your system. Be conscious of which thoughts are choosing to hold on to – are they mostly negative or positive?

Make a vow to hold onto the positive ones and release the negative thoughts back into the universe. When you begin to feel negative emotions or have negative thoughts, immediately cut your negative thought from your mind and swap it with a positive one. Ask yourself, what is good about this situation, thing, or person?

HOW CAN I stop having re-occurring negative thoughts about the past and stop letting them fog up the present?

I like is to write down ALL your negative thoughts of the past. Puke it onto a piece of paper. It's hard, but writing down negative thoughts from the past is one of the best ways to release them back into the universe. Throw your thoughts away or place them into the recycle bin in order to let them go and not look back. Do not complain about this past. This will allow you to become more present.

In addition, surround yourself around positive people. Get rid of the negative people from your life. There are many places to make friends as this world has become globalized and highly connected. You can make friends on Facebook (where I've made some of my best friends) and hangout together using Skype or Google Hangouts. Or if you want to meet someone in person, join a meetup group according to something your interested in or curious about at www.meetup.com.

HOW LONG DOES the present last? How do I

know when I'm drifting into the future so I can make an effort to pop back into the present?

I wish I could say that we had complete control over our subconscious mind, and could automatically control every thought and action we make, but I can't. It takes practice to remain present, and not get distracted by noises surrounding us, people dancing beside us, or cold memories from the past. It takes effort to move forward with feelings of anxiety running through our veins.

The present lasts as long as you allow it to, and the mind must be trained to relax, accepting "what is". Two primary emotions remove your mind from the present moment, those of which are fear for the future, and regret from the past.

So things didn't go exactly as planned. So what? Usually things don't go EXACTLY as planned, although it is often close to perfect (or good enough). As for getting past fear (or anxiousness) for the future, there is only one way to get past it. Take Nike's advice: Just DO it!

Many people fail to stay present and hop into feelings of fear for the future with new situations such as: first dates, job interviews, or talking to strangers. Once you drift into the future or past, you will feel fearful or wish that you would've said or done something differently. When this happens, get back in the present moment by taking a few seconds to close your eyes, smile, and focus on your breathing.

Ask yourself, what do I love about this moment? What am I grateful for in this moment? Breathe in the moment until you feel it.

HOW CAN I plan things and create a vision to be proactive and organized without living in the

future – as in how can I plan while at the same time live in the moment?

Use your knowledge from the past and your imagination to dream of a vision for your future. Design an action plan by creating small steps to reach your vision. This will create a sense of organization so that you won't have to use your present moment's energy having to remember how you can reach your vision.

After the plan for your vision is created, use your present moments to fully enjoy and embrace the process of getting to your goal or dream. Take your time to enjoy and take in each moment, fully tasting your foods, completely hearing the sounds around you, and totally seeing what is in front of you.

HOW CAN I focus intently on the delicious prime rib and the beautiful woman who made it instead of thinking about what is on my phone?

Do not take your phone with you when you are with the beautiful woman or eating the delicious prime rib. Keep your phone in another room, or give it to a friend to hold on to, forcing yourself to enjoy what is in front of you, as opposed to feeling anxious about what is on your phone.

BY NECESSITY the present needs to include aspects of the past and future – how can I see the balance between them and how should they be scheduled into one's present activities?

The past is there for a reason – to learn from, and make sense of things. Let it consume 10% of your thoughts. The future is there for a reason – to design your life by creating goals and dreams. Do you dream to travel to other countries and experience new cultures? Do you dream to own a business? Do you dream to write a book? Each of these can be done by placing them into your future - perhaps on a goal list (that you look at daily) or a vision board. As you strive to achieve your goals, enjoy the process, embrace it, and completely take in each new experience.

As for balance, life is a constant balancing match. There will be days when your past weighs heavier than your present, or when your future weighs more than your past. It depends on several factors, including the people you surround yourself around during the day, the amount of work you do during the day, and the amount of sleep you get each the day.

WHAT IS the best way to leave a lasting positive impact on ones children while living in the present moment?

Lead by example. It's the best way to teach your children. Show your children that you live a life of peace and joy in the present moment, taking in every experience as it is given to you. If you want your children to not regret the past, take on the perspective that "everything happens for a reason", and show your children how to use the past to learn from, not to dwell in.

I AM TRYING SO hard to eat healthy and live a healthy life. How do I know what is truly healthy for me?

I am not a nutritionist or a doctor but I will provide you with what I have learned from my experience. It is important to listen to your body and be aware of how it makes you feel when you eat particular foods. I suggest that you keep a log of every food you eat and how each of the foods (or meals) make your body and mind feel for 30 days. Then go back and assess which foods are good for your body. Do the foods make you feel more energetic or more lethargic? Do they make you feel hungrier or satisfy your appetite?

GIVEN the internal and external pressure to successfully meet personal and professional deadlines and commitments, how do we do everything and still live in the present moment?

It is important to set goals and take small action steps to reach your deadlines, while embracing the present moment. Pressure and consequences are often used to get things done faster (not necessarily better), and can be used as an extra adrenaline rush to get things done even when you thought you were maxed out.

HOW CAN peace be achieved in a world with so much hate and loathing?

The world is filled with racism, hate, and destruction. At the same time it is filled with just as much love, peace, and beauty. It all depends on where you choose to focus your attention.

Your focus requires a perspective shift. How can you see the peace behind the darkness? How can you show the people around you to also see the good?

One answer, look for it. It can be difficult, but the peace starts with you. Once you change your perspectives and find the peace within yourself, your view of the world will change.

Also, my personal suggestion is to avoid watching the news or reading the newspaper because that is where much of the hatred is found. It causes the world to believe that there is much more hatred and evil in the world than there actually is. The majority of the world's population has good intentions, and there are far less people that are filled with hatred and loathing than we have been programmed to believe.

Also, what you put out into the world, you will get back. Therefore, if you put out positive energy into your universe, you will get it in return. For instance, if you are friendly and smile at someone, they will be more likely to feed off your energy and smile back. The same goes with negativity. If you have an angry tone of voice when talking to someone, you can expect to get that back.

HOW CAN I live peacefully when the economy is unstable?

Do not rely on the economy. You have to step outside of the box. Talk to strangers. Meet people online. Join mastermind groups that are based around making money and financial security. There are hundreds, if not thousands of Facebook groups that are surrounded around making money and being successful.

TODAY WE HAVE SO many choices as we enjoy life. We have risen about laboring to find and prepare our food; to do our housework, make our clothes, etc. Communication and travel are instant...Therefore how can we encourage our youth to look beyond the man made and be

mindful of the natural beauty of this wonderful planet?

I feel overwhelmingly grateful for the blessings we've been given. This is the best time to live because of all the opportunity and knowledge we have, especially with the Internet allowing us to access information in seconds and connect us to people all the way across the world.

We can show our youth by our own example. I mention this quite a bit, but it is one of the best ways to teach others, especially our youth. We need to first embrace the natural beauty of the planet and then show our children. I suggest teaching children using gratitude and appreciation.

Everyday name three non-manmade things that you are grateful for, such as the ability to spend time with your child, the beautiful tree outside your home, and the birds that sing songs every morning. Then have your child name three non-man made things he or she is grateful for to help them be mindful of the natural beauty of our planet.

WHAT IS the formula to making living in the moment a reality?

Keep this formula in the back of your mind: 10% Past, 10% Future, 80% Present. It takes continuous effort from your conscious mind to remind yourself to stay present. Eventually, it will enter your subconscious mind, so you don't have to think about it as much.

I recommend setting up reminders, such as screen savers on your phone or computer, necklaces, bracelets, or rings that you can use to bring you back to the present once you begin to drift into the past or future.

A strategy I learned from the Coaches Training Institute, when I was training to become a life coach is to create an Avatar, or Captain. It is a powerful way to both stay in the present moment, and get answers by being playful (or even child-like). Some people consider this process a way of "putting on a different hat", or if you want to get fun, playful, and a bit ridiculous you can use an imaginary character (an Avatar), that you can take everywhere you go to give you advice, ask you powerful questions, and realign yourself with the present moment – almost like an inner source of wisdom. I encourage you to create an Avatar who will be your "best buddy" that pops up when you are in stressful situations where you need some assistance or wisdom.

Let's take a few minutes to create your Avatar. Close your eyes. Imagine blackness. And have a funny character all of a sudden pop out. What shape is it (he or her)? What color is it? What is its texture? Give it a name. What is it saying? This is your ally, your partner who you will give a ticket to join you on the ride of life. Just be sure that you discover something that resonates with you.

I named mine Guru. He looks like a golden, cartoon-like candlestick with 5 candleholders. The stems are not lit, but when he is happy the candle flames light up.

So, who is your avatar?

Use your Avatar to give you strategies and ask as you questions to help you stay present, peaceful, and happy. Take your Avatar wherever you go to keep you in check.

HOW CAN I forget and let go of the past, i.e. mistakes made in life?

You can't necessarily forget about the past, although you can let go of it. Here is an effective method that works.

Close your eyes. Take a look at your past, completely

replaying it in your mind. Play it as if it were a movie from start to finish.

Now take a moment to freeze-frame it. If it is color, turn it to black and white. Now shrink the image. Shrink it more. And more. And more until you only see a tiny dot. Now with your eyes still closed, grab it, squash it in your hand, and chuck it as far as you can. Now dust off your hands.

How do you feel now? If it comes back, repeat this process.

WHY DO our minds resist the present moment and rather, almost mechanically, prefer to dwell in the past and worry about the future?

It is the way we as humans are designed. If we could be completely in the present, we would be animals. It goes back to the caveman days of survival and replication. We needed to learn from our past trials and errors to survive. And we needed to think of our futures and replicate in order for our species to survive.

AM I REALLY HERE NOW?

If you're not here, then you're there. I find it challenging for me to be in the moment if I am exhausted due to lack of sleep. Otherwise, I believe that it is possible to be "here" and in touch with your body (which is always present and "here now") if you choose to.

Ask yourself, "Where am I?" And if the answer is, "I'm here!" then you know you're on the right track.

DOES one want to only live in the moment with no

Happiness

short and long term memory? Won't we be motivated by pure instant gratification only?

The present moment and instant gratification can be good, although it can also be destructive (i.e. excessive alcohol, drugs, promiscuous sex, etc.) if you were to permanently remain in the present moment. As mentioned before, the past is needed to learn from your mistakes, and the future is designed for you to dream.

WHY DO things happen the way they happen?

Both horrible and amazing things happen every day. Each person on this earth needs to dig deep and discover a purpose for "why" things happened the way they did.

HOW DO I stay focused on today when I am worried about tomorrow?

Here is a quick list of things you can do to stay focused on today:

1. Name and *feel* grateful for at least three things
2. Meditate for at least 12 minutes
3. Close your eyes and pay attention to your breathing
4. Take a minute to ask, "Where am I?"
5. Focus on your present environment. Look where you are seated, the place you are in, where your hands and feet are located, what each body part of yours is touching.
6. Make a "realistic" list of three things you want to accomplish today, and fully embrace the process of each of them during the day.

ISN'T it better to ask why not instead of why (a twist on the positive to negative)?

Both are important. I found "why not?" to be less threatening with more of a "take action" view behind it.

Whereas if somebody asks you "why?" it can often be perceived as judgmental, making people defensive. I prefer to replace "why" with "how come".

Although, "why" is the best question you can ask yourself because that is often the strongest motivation to get something done.

HOW DO you live in the present with a person who continues to twist and throw horrible events of the past in your face only to hurt you?

If possible, remove that person from your life because they are not adding value to your life. However, if you can't remove the person from your life, do the opposite and, although extremely difficult, fully love the person back. Write the person a heartfelt letter or explain to him (or her) how you feel, and why you feel that way (DO NOT write or speak it in an attacking way because the person will get defensive and the nonsense will continue). Explain to the person who you are now, and you can even include the person you are becoming. Remember, the past is over and you cannot change it, but you can let it go.

AT THE GRAND old age of 86, how do I learn to live alone?

Make friends who you can enjoy life with. Join local communities using www.meetup.com, or looking for groups to join on the Internet or newspaper.

Also, take the perspective that this is YOUR time to live. Do everything as if it were your first time, using all your senses. Feel things to your fullest. See things as clearly as possible. Hear sounds like you've never heard them before. Touch things as if you haven't

touched them before. Taste things as if you were tasting them for the first time. Experience EVERY MOMENT to it's fullest.

IN ORDER TO ACHIEVE HAPPINESS, success and fulfillment, I consider self-awareness as a main thing to master. How do I master self-awareness?

Self-awareness, the present moment, and mindfulness are all linked to each other, as they all have to do with being aware of your current state of mind and complete awareness of your body. Once you embrace one, the others are easier to achieve. Happiness requires living in the present moment. Use the future to dream of goals in order to achieve success, and the past to look back at your mistakes and grow.

HOW DO you keep your attention on the present when feelings, specifically anger and frustration, take hold of you?

When this happens, you must take a step back, get out of your head, and re-center yourself with the present moment. Fear of loss is the primary thing that causes anger and frustration. Those emotions do not exist when you are fully present. Fear exists with a future mindset. Again, to re-center yourself with your body, pause for a moment, fully taking in a few deep breaths so that as you inhale you can feel your stomach expanding. Feel your body beginning to relax and bring you back to a present state of mind.

In addition, make an effort to wipe away any frown

from your face, and force a smile because a smile can cause an incredible energy shift. Ask yourself, is it worth my energy to be angry and frustrated about this situation? Can you control it? If you can't, then there is nothing you can do but accept it, so of course it is not worth your energy or your health.

HOW DO I put aside all the mental stress, clutter, etc., to be able to focus on the "now" of everything? I struggle with this all day, everyday and it is the root of my anxiety disorder.

Release your mental stress or clutter by either dumping it all on a piece of paper. Afterwards, you can either put it into the recycle bin or if it important refer back to it later put it in a safe place to refer back to later.

In today's world, there are so many things we "need" to get done that it is easy to feel like a hamster racing around in a spin-wheel. I use Google calendars to organize all the clutter in my mind, and stay present. Every morning I look at what I have to do that day. If something pops in my head while I'm working on something else, I will add it to the calendar to get it off my mind. Then later that day (or the next morning) I can look back at it.

If it is unnecessary talk in my head that is blocking my peaceful present moment, I write all the mental stress down or talk-text it into my smart phone and trash it later because it is pointless to hold on to negative mind-clutter.

HOW DO I balance future ambitions, past reflections, and appreciate the present moment with the benefits we gain from each of these and consequences for lack of balance?

Past reflections and future ambitions are needed for every person to grow and dream. Although, the present moment is where you will find peace and joy. Think of things you are grateful for. They can range from anything from your health, to your ability to breathe, to your car that gets you from point A to point B.

Take a second to genuinely feel gratitude and appreciate what you have. If you have trouble accessing these feelings, then imagine what your life would be like if you were terminally ill, had to rely on a respirator to breathe, and didn't have a car. Now take a moment to think of three things you appreciate in your life now.

Balance each day of your life by focusing your time accordingly: 10% Past, 10% Future, and 80% Present. If you were to only have an hour each day, spend 6 minutes to dream of what you want from the next hour, 6 minutes to absorb what you've learned from your past, and 48 minutes in the present moment to fully enjoy and appreciate what you are doing and where you are now.

HOW DOES LIVING in the present moment tie into self love, especially if you come from a place of not loving yourself or thinking you're not worthy?

Humans are way too hard on themselves. It is partially because of other's expectations (your parent's, friends, boss, etc.) that have been ingrained into our minds. We sometimes feel that we are insignificant if we can't make a certain amount of money, be more attractive, or be smarter. Unworthiness is a feeling that we get when our minds drift to the past or future. If you are spending the majority of your time in either of these two, it will be hard to feel love for yourself.

Self-love is found in the present moment. Take a second to look at the incredible arms, hands, and fingers you've been given; the fully functioning legs, and feet you have that you can use to walk; the lungs you've been given to breathe; and the powerful mind you have been gifted with to dream, connect with others, and make sense of the past; or any of the other blessings you have. Now embrace all these qualities. Start new by taking this moment to be present, fully aware, and mindful of this moment and each of the moments you are given while you are alive on this earth.

Afterword

If you haven't already, take this moment to congratulate yourself for completing this section. You now have all the knowledge and understanding you need to live in the present moment.

Feel the texture of what your body is touching; see things with a new perspective – through lenses of complete curiosity and amazement. Listen to the sounds around you as if your ears had never heard sounds before. Feel and experience emotions to the fullest with every moment you are given.

Section III. Positive Thinking is the Gateway to Happiness

Section III. Positive Thinking is the Gateway to Happiness

Introduction

Have you ever entered a room, looked around it, and as you made eye contact with others, felt the energy shift to things like hostility, anger, and guilt? You can feel the negative emotions drain you, and you begin to feel your energy sucked right out of you. Now imagine stepping inside that same room, making eye contact, and feeling the energy shift to feelings of excitement, happiness, and comfort—feelings of positivity.

What if it could always be like this? What if these feelings were your own perceptions of the situation—meaning that the people were always neutral, but you had a preconceived view that people would be thinking negative thoughts about you? Imagine how good it would feel if you were able to flip these negative thoughts to positive ones so that people were always excited and happy to see you because you were filled with positivity. You would feel better and much more confident around people and, more importantly, you would feel much better being with yourself.

If positivity has the power to completely shift those

Introduction

feelings, imagine the effect it can have on you as an individual. If you allow yourself to have positivity at the core of who you are as a person, imagine how awesome life would be. Imagine how many people would enjoy being in your presence, how much happier you would feel going to work and even doing mundane tasks. Imagine how great it would feel to get out of a negative slump that's keeping you from moving forward in life.

Positivity brings so much more happiness into people's lives. It also brings more abundance and the power to attract more into your life including better people, more wealth, and improved inner thoughts. Many of the happiest and most successful people used the power of positive thinking. Some of these people include Dr. Wayne Dyer, Nelson Mandela, Benjamin Franklin, Mahatma Gandhi, and Isaac Newton.

Positive thinking needs to be a daily practice. It will not happen overnight. It needs to be a conscious effort of being aware of your thoughts and statements to determine if they are coming from a negative or a positive place. Being consciously aware of your thoughts before they can enter the unconscious mind and become a habit is the first step. It is believed that it takes 30 days of effort to form a habit. Therefore, if you take the steps and apply the strategies you'll read about in this book for a consistent 30 days, you will be well on your way to thinking more positively, feeling happier, and attracting more into your life.

20

The Road to Positivity

"Keep your thoughts positive because your thoughts become your words. Keep your words positive because your words become your behavior. Keep your behavior positive because your behavior becomes your habits. Keep your habits positive because your habits become your values. Keep your values positive because your values become your destiny."

-Mahatma Gandhi

EVERYTHING HAPPENS for a reason and many things can change your life. They can knock you down or they can lift you up, but at the end of the day it all depends on you. It's all in your mind. You, your neighbor, your workmates, and your friends all experience the same thing, but what makes it different is how you accept, react to, and view the circumstances.

Every human experience has two dimensions, just like a coin with two sides. It has both a negative component and a positive one, and one weighs heavier than the other, each one bearing different results. When you flip a coin and hold it in your hand, you only see one side, but it doesn't mean that you only have one option. There is another side that exists, and it is up to you to flip it around to train yourself to become a positive thinker.

For example, if you did not get hired during your job interview, there are two things that you can do. You can give up the job hunt, tell yourself that you are a failure, stop hoping that you will be successful in your career, and stay right where you are. Or, you can exit the interview room, hold your head high, and tell yourself that the job isn't right for you; you will get something better. With this, you can go on to look for another job, hoping to succeed in your endeavor. If you choose the first, you automatically lose the chance for success. It is depriving you of the opportunity to be happy. The opposite is true for the second option. Choosing the second option means taking steps to bring you closer to your goal.

When you have been going through something negative for a long period of time, such as a divorce or a "hopeless" job hunt, you've surely heard people telling you that there is a light at the end of the tunnel. This cliché statement is true. The bad will not last forever, and you need to have hope.

Believing that a positive thing can come out of something negative is not easy. It may sound miraculous even, and people have the tendency to be skeptical about it. How can a bad thing yield a good thing? The thing is that what you are going through is not really negative. The negativity of it all is just a product of your mind. It will only become negative once you let yourself believe that it is.

Though it is also true that optimism is not something that can be achieved overnight, it is something that you can achieve with time and practice. You may have been thinking that optimism is just a matter of the mind. Well, there's some truth to that, but not entirely. Optimism is also something that you do and say. It can be developed with the words you choose to use and the thoughts you choose to let enter your mind.

FOCUS on your goal

In everything that you do, nothing will bring you closer to your goal than focusing on it. Always keep your goal in mind so you don't lose your way. When you fail the job interview, don't think of it as losing your chance to succeed. Keeping the goal in mind will help you stay motivated as you work for it. For example, maybe you need to get a job to support yourself and your family, buy a house, get that car you've dreamed about for years, etc. What is your motivation?

Focus gives you direction, and when you know where you are going, even if you get lost along the way, you will still get back on track. Remember how people tell you that it's better late than never? It practically means the same thing here. The ability to remind yourself of why you are doing something has power in itself and can reenergize you.

GRATITUDE

Gratitude goes a long way. I believe gratitude and happiness are closely tied together. When you're grateful for things or qualities you possess, you're much more likely to create happiness in your life. For example, you might be grateful for the conversation you had yesterday with a friend or relative, or you might be grateful for your ability to communicate effectively with your co-workers, explaining how your ideas are imperative to the success of a particular project. Even being grateful for the things people take for granted, such as food to eat or the ability to walk or being loved, can bring in a refreshing sense of joy and happiness.

Happiness is not always getting what you want when you want it. Often times, it means being content and appreciating what you have. This might get you asking how in the world you can appreciate something like blowing a job interview. It does not mean you're a failure; it simply means that you were not the person they were looking for and that there is something better out there for you.

Maybe you can think of the interview as practice, and with each interview you have you will get more confident; maybe you learned something from the interaction or from your experience that you can be grateful for, which can help you to improve for your next interview.

CONDITION yourself

For a machine to function properly, it needs conditioning. Your body, in order to function optimally, needs a warm-up every morning. This principle holds equally true in the way you live your life. That is where a ritual or routine can make a world of difference. What are a few things you can do to condition yourself to be happy every morning?

A few examples might include doing 50 jumping jacks to feel energized and get your blood flowing, being grateful for being alive and breathing, or positive affirmations to remind you of the amazing qualities you have.

BE Persistent and Resilient

Life is a journey. If you don't keep moving, you'll get left behind. Always push yourself to try out new things and challenge yourself to keep moving forward even when times get tough. There may be obstacles along the way, but you can always knock them down. You are naturally creative and resourceful. You will find your way around them, and you have the ability to overcome them.

DON'T JUST REACT; respond

Reaction is an immediate response to a situation. It is like a reflex that is automatic when you encounter something. When you accidentally touch a hot stove, you reflexively remove your hands from it. Though this reflex is a natural protective mechanism of the body, not everything can be managed with a simple reflex. Sometimes, to be able to protect yourself, you must think first before acting, or respond instead of react.

When you are hungry, you react by grabbing any food that you see. When you respond, you think of ways to get food in the shortest time possible and to avoid being hungry in the future. If you want to be an optimistic person, it is not enough that you just react to the situation. Don't just cry, or give up, or stop moving. Respond to every failure by thinking of ways that you can succeed the next time you encounter the same adversity. That is how we grow as individuals.

21

Ways to a Stress-Free Life

"Adopting the right attitude can convert a negative stress into a positive one."

-Hans Selye

Many people don't see the good side of things because they are too preoccupied dealing with their worries, fears, anxieties, and stressors. Stress has always been perceived as something negative, but it is so ironic that people always seem to look for things to stress about. When they wake up in the morning, they think of what they are going to wear, how they are going to reach their office in the fastest possible way, who they are going to have lunch with, and what time they can get back home. These simple things may seem so uncomplicated and benign, but the truth is they can cause great worry and unnecessary stress.

No matter what you do, and no matter how you try to

avoid it, stress will always be there, waiting around the corner for you to come and get it. In fact, you need it to function properly. For example, you are preparing for an exam or work presentation tomorrow and you are feeling some stress about it. To relieve some of the stress, you study and prepare for it. Though stress here is something that you don't see as positive, your response to it is. The next thing you know, you did very well on the exam or presentation! Imagine if you are not worried about your exam. The most likely thing you'd do is not prepare for it. Sometimes, not feeling the stress is more dangerous because you don't perceive any harm.

Stress takes on different forms. It can be mild, which is something that you can easily overcome, or it could be something more severe, something that can exhaust you of your energy and resources. Mild stress, just like the example given above, is helpful because it keeps you prepared for what's going to happen. But if the stress is so severe that you don't know what to do anymore, then it becomes harmful.

When you feel that you can no longer perform well in your job, or you can no longer think straight, or you think that you are not getting the results that you want to achieve anymore, you are likely undergoing severe stress. At this point, it is not advisable to continue with what you are doing. Just like a machine that has been used excessively, people function inefficiently when they are under severe stress. Eliminating the stressors is not easy, but there are ways you can do it.

DON'T TRY to control everything

People have the tendency to want to control everything: their time, money, and other people. What they don't know is that most of their stress comes from trying to control everything. It's not bad to be carefree every once in a while. Give yourself some freedom by not thinking about your bills at home, your work deadlines, and the traffic jam outside. Recognize that, at the moment, these things are out of your control.

You can avoid thinking about them. Change your mindset. You can use the analogy of a dresser. In the bottom drawer, you can store all your stresses and worries. In the top drawer, you can store all your happy thoughts and things you're grateful for. If you're having difficulty changing your mindset or thoughts, go ahead and place them in the bottom drawer and grab something from the top one.

SPEND one hour a day without technology

It is true that technology plays an important role in people's lives. However, it is also true that it takes up a large part of one's time. People are meant for interaction and socialization. Though technology, like smartphones, tablets, and computers is meant for communication, people nowadays forget and do not seem to bother talking with their classmates, coworkers, and neighbors. It is as if their minds have been taken over by their devices.

These gadgets can be a source of additional stress. Spending one hour a day (or longer) without them would be a helpful way of relieving your stress. It can be very challenging for some to not check their email or look at their phone for even one hour. Instead of interacting with your smartphone or computer, talk with the people around you. Laugh out loud with them and share stories with them. You'll see how refreshing and energizing this can be.

For more information on strategies for telling stories, and strategies for talking to strangers and making new friends, check out: The Storytelling Method and The Conversation Method, which will give your social life a new set of wings.

TAKE a Time Out

Time out is for those who are brave enough to take a step back and rethink everything. Taking a time out does not mean giving up; it just means that there are some things that you need to take care of before proceeding to the next step. In a sense, it's a way to unwind, look at the big picture, and refocus on what is important about whatever you are currently working on.

Stress often results from too much work and not giving your body or mind enough time to relax. Give yourself a break from working. Taking short breaks each hour increases productivity. Even a short 2-5 minute break to stretch your body, or 5 minutes to walk around or step outside and get some fresh air will help. When you continue working despite exhaustion, you may produce unsatisfactory results that can further aggravate your stress. Some people like to meditate, and others like to take a walk to clear their mind. So, go ahead and take that time out.

LIVE in the present moment

Most of the anxiety, worry, and stress that you feel arises from thinking about the future or the past. You stress about "what ifs". What if you did this or what if you did not do that? You worry whether it's going to rain or whether you can meet the deadline of your assignment. Live in the present so that much of your worry and anxiety will be eliminated. A rule I like to use is the 80/20 rule—spend 80% of your time enjoying the present moment, and 20% thinking about the future or what you can learn from your past. Life is most fun and relaxing when you are enjoying the present moment.

22

Build Your Confidence

"With everything that has happened to you, you can either feel sorry for yourself or treat what has happened as a gift. Everything is either an opportunity to grow or an obstacle to keep you from growing. You get to choose."

-Dr. Wayne W. Dyer

People have different views on how confidence is built. Some believe it comes from being popular in school or at work. For others, it comes from being beautiful or handsome, or being the richest in town. Or, it could mean being able to accomplish something or being a member of a certain group of people. If you are going to use these definitions of confidence, it seems that it is directly associated with material and physical things. The reality is that confidence comes from within, and through this all the external things can be achieved.

Confidence is not something that only refers to a certain aspect of a person; rather, it refers to the wholeness of the person—the physical, emotional, and intellectual aspects, as well as strengths and weaknesses. Appreciating who you *really* are and being able to proudly walk out into the world with *all* your attributes, both good and bad, is the real essence of self-confidence.

The advantage of improving your self-confidence is not only about being able to do *what you want*, but also it gives you a positive attitude. Imagine yourself being appointed as a leader in a team, given that you had all the qualifications. At the same time, imagine that you do not believe in yourself and are not confident in your abilities. It is likely that you would refuse the position. You would fear that you could not fulfill the responsibilities associated with leadership due to your lack of self-confidence. You would still have all the qualifications and abilities to do it, but you would resist.

You may not be the best leader at first, but you will be and your confidence will grow as you gain more experience with the position. Confidence is built from practicing something over and over again.

On the other hand, if you are already the type of person who is confident, knowing that you have the ability and the capacity to become a leader, then you would most likely accept the position and the responsibilities associated with it. With improved self-confidence, you are able to lift your spirits and believe that you can accomplish whatever it is that you need to do.

Having good self-confidence can sometimes be equated with being strong and resilient. Everything that you do requires strength, not only physically, but mentally as well. The will to get out of bed early in the morning to go to work or school is already a sign of strength. You are able to overcome the temptation of just lying in your bed, going back to sleep, and spending the rest of the day being lazy. Being confident in what you do drives you to achieve your goals, work at your best, and overcome any challenges that come your way. When you are confident in who *you* are, you become stronger and more resilient to adversity.

5 TECHNIQUES TO BUILD CONFIDENCE:

1. **Be Realistic**

Low self-confidence often stems from setting goals and expectations that are too high or unrealistic. Though it is helpful to aim high, it is also important to keep your goals realistic, keeping in mind *your* strengths and weaknesses. If you want to buy a house and lot worth $1,000,000 and you are earning just $5,000 a month, it is not realistic to say that you can buy that property within a few months.

When you are not able to achieve your goal within the time frame you set, there's a tendency to get discouraged and unmotivated. This will cause your self-confidence to go down. Therefore, set realistic goals, even if they seem super small, because there is a sense of fulfillment from achieving goals. Again, I encourage you to set big goals, but make them realistic. Even if you have to start with tiny steps, such as setting a day and time to make a budget, it will bring you closer to a realistic time frame of when you can buy a house or what house you can afford.

1. **Acknowledge Strengths and Accept Weaknesses**

YOUR SELF-CONFIDENCE IS FOUNDED on your strengths and weaknesses, and it is important for you to be aware of them. Know which of your characteristics need improvement and which ones you can use to your advantage. Working your way up does not stop with just knowing them; you have to use them, improve on them, and work with them. For example, you know deep down that you are a good leader. When the opportunity to lead comes your way, grab it and maximize your potential. Making use of your strengths will make you more aware of your abilities and give you the opportunity to keep improving. Meanwhile, it is also important that you don't ignore your weaknesses. The more you challenge your weaknesses and reflect on them, the faster you will improve.

1. **Don't Compare**

MOST PEOPLE LOVE COMPARING themselves with other people. What makes her better? What makes him the boss's favorite? What qualities do I not have that he has? These are just some of the questions that people ask whenever they see someone they think is better than them.

Comparing yourself with other people will just highlight your weaknesses more than your strengths. It's nonsense because everyone is good at certain things and bad at other things. No one is going to be good at everything.

Instead of comparing yourself with other people, you can compare your future self to the old one. One of the great things about emotions is that they are elastic and have the ability to change if we choose to do so. You can take note of your characteristics that you want to change, work on them for the next month, and then reevaluate yourself. Or, you can look at yourself now and compare yourself to who you used to be. If you were once very controlling and bossy, you can ask yourself whether you still are or not. If you were once a pessimistic person, you can check in with yourself and see if you are now an optimistic person. People change, and you are not an exception. Change for the better and don't compare yourself with other people.

1. **Praise and Reward Yourself**

NEGATIVE SELF-TALK usually arises when you feel that you are not loved or appreciated by the people around you. The reality is that you don't *need* them to make you feel better. Before looking for someone who can praise you, learn to praise yourself. Pat yourself on the shoulder or congratulate yourself for a job well done. After all, it is only you who knows how much effort and how much time you have invested. For example, when you have successfully closed a deal with your business partner, treat yourself to dinner or something special *for yourself*. Don't wait for someone else to congratulate you.

1. **Be Assertive**

PEOPLE SOMETIMES CONFUSE assertiveness with aggressiveness. Assertiveness is something admirable and positive, while aggressiveness can be perceived as more negative. Being aggressive is often seen as achieving your goals in whatever way you can, even if it includes harm to others. On the other hand, assertiveness is achieving your goal with consideration for the people involved, making sure that no one gets hurt along the way.

A simple scenario showing the differences between being passive, aggressive, and assertive could be this: you are in a hurry walking through a crowded street and someone stands in your way. There are three possible things that can happen. You can either push or shout at the person and demand that he moves, say nothing and hope that he moves, or you can say, "Excuse me," and wait for the person to move aside. Of course, the first one might be the faster way but may cause harm. The second would likely be ineffective, whereas the latter is the better option because you get what you want without causing harm to others. If you want to achieve something, assert yourself. This is the way to get the most effective result.

23

Bring On Positivity

"Man often becomes what he believes himself to be. If I keep on saying to myself that I cannot do a certain thing, it is possible that I may end by really becoming incapable of doing it. On the contrary, if I have the belief that I can do it, I shall surely acquire the capacity to do it even if I may not have it at the beginning."

-Mahatma Gandhi

Optimism is not just a state of the mind; it is also shown through your actions and words. If your work gets canceled due to inclement weather, an optimistic person would enjoy the time off or work on something else to be productive. Positivity is about having a positive attitude even when challenging situations arise. One psychologist once theorized that you attract what you think about most. This is the Law of Attraction, and it says that when you think of and focus on something, it will happen. Remember how you wished to not see a certain person and then you did? You focused your thoughts and energy on that particular person, and there they were! Well, that's the Law of Attraction.

This theory is true whether you are thinking negative *or* positive thoughts. The *more* you think of negative thoughts, the *more* you'll encounter negative things. Let's look at this scenario. Imagine you're in a taxi hurrying your way to work with a traffic jam on the street. Human nature tells you to start worrying because you might be late to work. When you do, you decide to get out of the cab and power-walk your way through the traffic jam. As you are walking, you keep looking at your watch, ticking and ticking. Twenty minutes until work became ten, then rapidly became five. At this point, you're stressed and sending out all types of negative energy. As you cross the street while looking at your watch, a car hits you. It may not be a big hit but you still feel the pain. And because you are very anxious and stressed during that time, you shout at the driver and confront him. Now the clock says you are late. With this scenario, you can see that a cascade of events will happen once you strongly think negative thoughts.

The same is true when you think of more positive thoughts. When you are about to enter your workplace, you start telling yourself that you can do all your tasks for the day. You greet everyone with a smile on your face, find your way to your desk and pleasantly start working. Even if a pile of unfinished papers greets you that morning, you do not panic. Instead, you look at each of them and prioritize them. You group all papers needing immediate attention and you do the same for the not-so-urgent ones. With a positive attitude, you gradually finish them all without undue stress.

Adopting positivity, just like other processes, takes time. You need to consciously make an effort to practice it every moment of every day, whatever comes your way, until it becomes a good habit. Again, it is believed that it takes 30 days of consistently doing something to form a habit. Adopting positivity is a commitment, and you have to be faithful in adopting positivity not only in your thoughts, but also in your actions and words. Below are some strategies to begin with positivity.

BE healthy

Many people don't think they can manage their problems because they are sick or because they feel too weak to accomplish their tasks. If this is the case, the best way to counteract it is to stay healthy. Start a healthy lifestyle by eating a balanced and healthy diet, one that has the right amount of carbohydrates, proteins, and other sources that you need. A food regimen that contains plenty of vegetables and fruits is good because they contain vitamins and minerals that are essential for the proper functioning of your cells.

Exercise is another way of maintaining a healthy lifestyle. Exercise does not only make your body stronger and your muscles larger, but also is a good way of relieving stress and energizing yourself. If you exercise regularly, you'll have the zest to work the whole day. Without exercise or good nutrition, you'll often feel lazy, inadequate, and weak.

CHANGE the way you think

Though changing the way you think is as difficult as changing the way you were brought up, it is something that you can achieve over time. Emotions are things that we ultimately have control over, and we have the ability to change the way we feel about certain things. Much of it can be changed by a shift of perspective or the way we view certain situations. Think of ways to turn your negative thoughts into positive ones, and do not let these negative thoughts control you. Ask yourself, what is one positive thing I can take out of this negative perspective? Then, look for another positive thing and focus your energy on those positive things instead of the negative ones.

START **positive self- talk**

You don't *need* other people to encourage you. You can do it to yourself. A simple "Good job!" or "Congratulations!" can do the trick. Even better, with this method you don't need a specific time to do it. You can do this when you are busy, when you are not doing anything, or when you are eating. You don't need anyone to do this either. It may sound silly, but it works. Talk to yourself like you're talking to a friend: encourage yourself, praise yourself, and always remind yourself that you are powerful enough to overcome all the challenges that you will encounter in the future.

If you are doing something for the first time, don't be afraid. Negative self-talk may sound like, "I don't know how to do this," but positive self-talk would say, "This is a new experience and I will learn new things from this." If you want to do something but you don't have the resources, negative self-talk would say, "I **cannot** do it because I need this first." Positive self-talk would most likely be, "I **can** do it. I just need to get this first."

ALWAYS LOOK FORWARD **to something**

Every day, you get to encounter different challenges,

experience various events, or meet new people. When you see the things happening to you as being part of something great, then you are attracting positive things into your life.

Positivity and optimism start with a positive attitude. You can gain optimism by anticipating that something good will come out of whatever it is you are going through right now.

24

Half Empty or Half Full?

"Optimism is the most important human trait, because it allows us to evolve our ideas, to improve our situation, and to hope for a better tomorrow."

-Seth Godin

When people see a glass half-filled with water, they can see it as either half full or half empty. Seeing a glass as half empty is a sign of negativity, while seeing a glass half full is the opposite. The way you perceive this scenario reflects how you perceive your life. Take a moment and think about how you perceive the glass. Is it half full or half empty?

If you see the glass as half full, it means that you are on your way to positive thinking. It may not be as fast as pouring water into the glass until it overflows, but it is something that you can achieve with time. If you see the glass as half empty, it means that you believe there is

Happiness

nothing you can do to take control of your life. However, if your glass is half empty, the good news is that it is possible to change, as all emotions are flexible or elastic.

At the end of the day, when you look back on the things that have transpired or the things that you have learned, you have the choice to see the glass as half empty or half full. It is your choice and no one else's.

Positivity is complex and does not work without the presence of the other parts. You need to be positive not only in your thoughts, but also in your words and actions. All these elements must work together to achieve complete optimism. Thinking positively without acting positively is useless. It is like knowing what you want but not taking action to get it. Words are equally important because they form emotions and either help or hinder you in challenging situations.

Positive self-talk is a form of catharsis that helps you express your emotions and be aware of them. Once you have acknowledged your emotions, you can easily find a way to address them. Then you can let go of the negative impacts of your experiences and put a more positive tone to it.

Everything is a matter of perspective. It is up to you to make the choice of how you respond to life. If you choose negative, you will lose. If you choose positive, you'll flourish.

Afterword

A positive attitude teaches you that anything is possible. With positivity, you are confident and more willing to take on new challenges. You are ready to face the world, and you will not be afraid to conquer your fears.

I encourage you to read this section again and use it as a reminder of how you can continue to implement a positive mindset. It is one of the greatest strategies that we as humans can develop and train ourselves to do.

It may not be easy to remain positive, especially when tough situations arise, but remember that you have power over your emotions, and you are the only one who can control what you are doing, how you feel toward situations, and how you respond to others.

Continue to make positive thinking a daily practice until it becomes a habit, which—as stated previously—takes 30 days of conscious effort to form.

Section IV. Program Your Mind to Be Happy

Section IV. Program Your Mind to Be Happy

Introduction

Neuro-linguistic programming (NLP) is a field of study in psychology that unlocks human potential by changing the way we see things. It solves our problems by shifting our perspectives so that we can improve our lives (Witkowski, 2010). What follows is a change in language or replacing a word used in a sentence to completely shift the emotion or feeling produced by the sentence.

Changing how we perceive and identify ideas will change how our mind reacts (or responds). Our brain is programmed to react to various phenomena simply by recalling concepts based on habits, patterns, and strategies. NLP techniques can be used to change these habits to get the results we desire (Dilts, 1980).

Neuro-linguistic programming (NLP) was pioneered in the 1970s by a linguistic specialist named John Grinder and a Gestalt therapist named Richard Brandler. They theorized that our minds are tied closely to our language and behavior. Their techniques were proven effective against stage fright, phobias, and anxiety (Hofmann, 2009). However, NLP is not limited to solving phobias and anxi-

Introduction

ety. Its biggest use is in the field of interpersonal relationships to communicate more effectively.

NLP has shown people how to adapt to various personality types, creating more rapport, harmony, and friendships. It has improved our ability to connect with each other so that we can understand each other on a deeper level. For example, it allows you to adjust the type of language you use in order to connect with a person, whether the person is a visual, kinesthetic, or auditory learner, simply by watching their eye movements.

NLP has also shown us that *we* are the biggest solution to any challenge we may be facing. You have the ability to *choose* to let your emotions work for you or against you. Problems are caused by choices and decisions that have already been made, and the right mindset can often relieve us of any disappointment, anger, and stress.

Each person has created their own vision of the world with their five senses. Our senses create a mental map out of the things we see, hear, taste, smell, and touch. These mental maps are how we perceive the world. However, this perception isn't factual, or the true reality. It is a subjective reality, which is the concept of varying perspectives.

An example of subjective reality is water. Swimmers will think about going towards the sea to enjoy the water. Others will stand in shock over the fear of drowning. Two subjective realities are revealed: water is an enjoyable place and water kills. The contrasting ideas happen because people have different backgrounds. The person with hydrophobia possibly had a near-death experience during childhood that they carried into adulthood. The swimmer, on the other hand, might have been taught how to swim at an early age and thus enjoys the sea.

1. How to Build Rapport

Introduction

Building friendship, harmony, and most importantly trust is the key to flourishing relationships. These are core components of building rapport, which is a sense of acceptance and trust. Having goodwill can make it easier for us to open up, connect, and have amazing interactions.

Everybody has a type of person they naturally click with or prefer to interact with. If communication between two people is not in sync, chances are they won't get along. At the same time, it is still easy to develop a strong relationship or build rapport with that person.

Mirroring

Essentially, mirroring is mimicking the behavior of the person you're talking to. Under the Law of Attraction, people easily bond with others that exhibit the same traits as they do. First impressions last, which is one of the reasons mirroring is such an important technique when first interacting with someone. Mirroring others makes it easier to understand other people's energies and build rapport (Clibby, 2004).

Mirroring is done best if it's subtle, as in not copying your subject's every movement from head to toe, but instead taking on or imitating some of the movements of the other person, such as their head position or arm movements. This might feel uncomfortable at first, but after doing it a few times you will get comfortable with it and the other person will appreciate it, whether they notice it or not.

1. **Match the body language**

If the person you're talking to has a straight posture, you should match it. If the person has their arms crossed, subtly cross yours. If their head is tilted slightly, tilt yours as well. Return the same gestures, like handshakes and smiles, to develop courtesy and trust. They will feel appreciated, loved, and more willing to open up.

1. Match breathing rhythms

The rhythm of your breath explains the energy that you are using. Slow breathing is a sign of calm and relaxed energy, while fast rhythmic breathing indicates an anxious or nervous state. How do you want to come across?

1. Match the tone of voice, rhythm, and tempo

Loudness indicates the intensity of emotions. A loud voice is a sign of anger and frustration, whereas a soft but audible one indicates calmness. How do you want to come across?

Pitch is the tone of your voice. A high pitch is perceived as exciting and a low one is associated with anger. It's kind of like a chihuahua. Serious but informal conversation, like a sales talk, uses a moderate pitch.

Rate refers to the speed of speaking. A gradual increase in rate signifies a rise in intensity. Too much rate, however, is a sign of nervousness. On the other hand, boredom or disinterest is associated with a slow rate.

Quality is your key to be understood. Pronunciation, articulation, and idiolect (personal manner of speaking) are things you need to keep in mind for effectively communicating.

Silence dictates the flow of your conversation. Match the silence that your partner gives you. Silence gives you the chance to listen and regroup.

Introduction

Caution should be used when mirroring. You don't want to look like a robot. Do not mirror *everything* your subject does in one go. Start with posture, then move to body language until you reach the stage of mimicking paralanguage. Whenever your subject does something, return the favor, but this time make the movement smaller. Rapport is all about matching the energy with the people you are interacting with.

Systemic processes of the environment and mind

Our minds are tightly interconnected with our environment. The various stimuli that we receive from the world are brought to our brains for interpretation. Afterwards, our minds create a perception about it, either negative or positive. Therefore, if you place a negative view on the situation, it will remain negative and you will only see the mistakes until you make the conscious effort to find the positives, or the things that went *right* about it. These perceptions become your reality.

One small request before we get too much further: use the power of NLP with integrity and good judgement, and if you are ever in doubt whether or not something is appropriate, reach out to a qualified NLP professional.

Filtering

In NLP, it is believed that every behavior has a positive intention (Ellerton, 2013). Although the positive intent may not be clear or even make sense according to someone else's view of the world, for the person engaging in the behavior, it makes sense in their reality. This understanding helps to explain why not everyone wants the same things in life or reacts in the same way to situations. This goes to show that we each have different perceptions, not that one of us is right and the other wrong.

Introduction

Even though you might not agree with another person's reality, it is important to not judge the person but rather to appreciate and respect that they have different beliefs and values from you. Respect that the other person may hear, see, feel, and perceive the world differently than you do. Therefore, he won't be driven by the same values or make the same choices as you.

For example, if you are talking with someone and all of a sudden he raises his voice at you, yells, or disappears into his bedroom, you might find this completely unacceptable behavior. Be curious about it. Take a look at it from his perspective. With his model of the world and his circumstances in life, perhaps he felt uncomfortable or overwhelmed in the conversation, and he felt that was the only option he had, or maybe he had difficulties with external factors in his life—for example, maybe his dog just died.

Your filters were developed and put it place from things like your family when you were growing up, your spiritual practice, any beliefs or values you hold from your country of origin, as well as any assumptions you've made about the world. If you don't like your current filters, beliefs, or habits, then you are the only person who has the power to change them.

First, you must become consciously aware of what they are attracting or detracting in your life. These are your perceptions of how you see the world, and it drives your emotions and your behaviors for how you respond to the world. This is your unique reality. If you want to get different results from your reality, NLP is about changing these beliefs.

Cause and effect

Many of us live our lives in effect—meaning that we blame others or circumstances for our bad moods and depend on others to feel good about ourselves. For example, you might think, "If only my spouse understood me better, I'd be happier." Well, you are the only one who can change that. Your spouse may not even know how you feel, or you may be resisting because you might be assuming that he or she doesn't care. If you continue to wait, nothing will change.

If you choose to be at cause, then you are making decisions and creating what you want in life. You are not relying on others for your happiness, and you understand that. While you can be supportive and cheer others to keep moving forward, you cannot take responsibility for others' emotional states. Doing so places a huge weight on your shoulders that can feel quite draining. With cause, you are taking responsibility for your actions–both the good and the bad. You know that you have choices and that the world is filled with opportunities to achieve what you *really* want (Ellerton, 2006).

Failing is the best feedback

Everyone will fail or make mistakes here and there. However, the thing that separates us is how we perceive it or how much we allow it to either positively or negatively affect us. In NLP, it is believed that there is no such thing as failure, just feedback. If something doesn't go as planned, it doesn't mean that you are a failure, it simply means that you've found something that doesn't work for you. It gives you an opportunity to learn how to improve and do better for next time. What if you were to view every failure as feedback?

25

The Body, the Mind, and NLP

"What's going on in the inside shows on the outside." -Earl Nightingale

We are always communicating, whether it be with words, tone of voice, facial expressions, posture, hand position, or choosing not to respond to a text message or email. When we first meet someone, we observe their body movements before speaking. We are currently sizing up each other, trying to figure out our personalities even before the first word.

As cliché as it may sound, actions speak louder than words. Research has found it takes 4 minutes to make a first impression. You only have that short amount of time to make a good impression. Surprisingly, we do not use words that much in creating that crucial first impression. Humans judge 55% based on body language. Paralanguage (manner of speaking) accounts for 38% and the content from our words is a mere 7%. Even our voice tone and rhythm is more important than what we actually say.

. . .

UNDERSTANDING how our minds work

Before we discuss the different body languages, we will briefly tackle how our brains are wired. The brain has two hemispheres. The left hemisphere of our mind is in charge of the logical data processing. It is the center of conscious thinking. On the other hand, emotions are triggered by activity in the right hemisphere. The right is also responsible for our intuition and creativity.

Since we are cross-wired, the right hemisphere controls the left side of the body, while the left brain controls the right side. It follows that any body language shown on any particular side corresponds to the brain hemisphere activating it. Any action done on the left side of the body connotes conscious actions, while the right side means unconscious actions (Bandler, 1993).

FACIAL LANGUAGE

Facial expressions are the first things we see in a person. Our moods can be quickly read depending on how relaxed or tense our facial muscles are. Even our eyelids are powerful means of communication.

- **Smiling**

WE CAN EASILY READ feelings using the mouth as a reference. A smile is associated with happiness and interest, although smiling too much can hide disinterest. Exaggerated smiling gives assurance or courtesy to the speaker that we are listening even if, in reality, we are not. A frown gives signs of sadness and dissatisfaction. Frowning is unlikely when people first meet, for we would rather hide our true sentiments than be rude. A straight expression indicates seriousness and neutrality. Think about what impression you want to give off next time you're speaking.

- **Chin**

Sentiments can also be seen by checking how we use our chin. Chin stroking is a sign of careful studying of data presented. People also perceive this as a gesture of skepticism. On the other hand, scratching connotes confusion.

- **Nostrils and Jaw**

Nostrils indicate temperament or mood. Heavy breathing and flaring nostrils are signs of anger. It is important to be aware of these signs. Approach these people in a soft and approachable tone. Don't force them to open up. Instead, allow them space for a few moments before engaging again.

Another indicator of temperament is the jaw muscles. The jaw usually goes in sync with the nostrils. Impatience and anger are signified by the flexing and pumping of the jaw muscles.

EYES DON'T LIE

Although eye expressions are part of facial non-verbal communication, they must be discussed in-depth.

Ophthalmics, the communication shown by eye movements, is an effective tool to detect mood or sentiments (Corballis, 2012). We are sometimes oblivious to the fact that eyes let out a lot of information.

- White areas showing below the iris (the colored

part of the eye) reveal the amount of stress being experienced by a person. White areas on the left eye reveal that there is stress in the right hemisphere. This means that the subject might be under stress from the body such as lack of sleep or food.

THE RIGHT EYE indicates stress from an external source. If white areas underneath the iris show after being exposed to stressful concepts like deadlines and overtime, the person might be receiving discomfort from those.

- Eyelids show the optimism of people. Watch the bottom lid to see the reaction of the person to your words. If the bottom lid is straight, the person is skeptical. Gaining the trust of a person will soon make the lid become rounded. This means that the subject is opening up to you and that rapport is established.

THE ARMS and hands

As we go down the body, we begin to read more about what a person feels. The hands are the primary tool of humans, thus we subconsciously use them to express our mood. These appendages contain more nerves connected to the brain than any other body part.

- The hands can show anxiety, restraint, or shyness if they are held together. This happens because the energy is being contained in

between them. Hence, this is a way to channel negative energy, such as anger and nervousness.
- If formed in a triangle shape, the hands exhibit a trait of confidence or deep thinking. A variation of this is a rhombus shape, when the thumbs are extended further towards the person. A popular figure that uses this gesture is German Chancellor Angela Merkel. The hand gesture has been named the Merkel rhombus. It creates a calm yet serious aura.
- Raising your arms while opening your palms will exhibit honesty and acceptance. The opposite implies defiance.
- When people show a contemplative look while using their hands to cover their mouths, they have ideas yet would rather keep them to themselves for now. Encourage people with this look to share their thoughts, for it might make the conversation more well-rounded.
- The manner of how we cross arms also displays our confidence. A partial crossing of the arms is a way for people to unconsciously soothe their nerves. People showing this behavior are feeling anxious. You can ease the mood by telling them jokes or making them laugh.

FULLY CROSSED arms show unwillingness to work and cooperate. If they are holding each other, it is an attempt to reserve one's internal feelings.

FOOT COMMUNICATION

The feet are often ignored in reading body language. However, the feet are more candid than any body gestures.

When people lie, they try to hide the evidence by altering their body movements. They focus on other features like the face, not realizing that their feet are a dead giveaway.

By observing how we sit, we can infer whether the person is either dominant or submissive. Men usually want to be viewed as dominant. That's why they take up a lot of space when sitting. They either sit in a figure four position or spread their legs apart. Women are more reserved, thus they cross their legs to take up the least possible space.

The legs also reveal the sincerity of a person while listening. When people are interested, their legs point towards the person with the feet off slightly in a 45-degree angle. However, if the legs are pointing towards the exit, this implies that the person is no longer interested in what you're saying. Be aware of the direction of your feet when communicating.

Reading people's body languages can help us decide how to approach a person in the friendliest and most approachable way.

3. Change Your Emotions with NLP

WE HAVE all experienced staring at the loads of work in front of us and feeling overwhelmed and lazy. We just can't get that kick start to get our minds moving. The problem is we usually think of our workload as a boring matter. Because of this association, our bodies respond by slowing our actions and inducing a sleep-like state. We lose motivation and we end up opening another internet tab to use social media. The work just piles up and we lose all hope.

Another situation is during a public show. When we are faced with an audience that is looking at us, we get anxious. Following the brain, the body reacts similarly, with fast shallow breaths and shaking legs. If this feeling carries on towards the performance, you might end up choking, as your emotions are completely controlling your body.

We can change our bodies' responses by shifting our emotions associated with work. Thus, we can become more productive. The technique used is called anchoring. It is a method of recalling previous positive experiences and associating them with the current situation (Dilts, 1980).

ANCHORING

Anchoring can be applied in many situations, like at work, before and during a presentation, before and during a job interview, performing on stage, meeting someone new, or asking someone out on a date. It can be likened to copying and pasting positive emotions as needed. In the process, we delete the negative feelings. You can do anchoring when you wake up, on your way to work, or minutes before you perform.

1. **Mental preparation**

FIRST, find a quiet place. In this technique, peace and serenity are key. Therefore, distractions need to be eliminated to maximize the effects of your mental exercises. Relax so that your heartbeat slows down, and breathe deep. Cancel your outer world by closing your eyes and focusing.

1. **Recall a positive experience**

Happiness

IT CAN BE ANYTHING, as long as this experience makes you feel good whenever you think of it. The memory might be when you first asked someone out on a date and the person happily accepted, or when you presented a report to your boss and got a positive response. Devote at least 10 seconds to remembering the details.

Humans are more effective if all 5 senses are activated. Let the mental pictures flow, and include the sounds and touches that were around. Do your best to relive what it actually felt like in that exact moment.

- What were the sounds around you?
- How did you feel?
- How did it smell?
- Where were you?
- What did it look like?
- Who else was around you?

1. **Associating with an action**

Keep the memory playing in your mind. While you are doing this, do an action. The most common action is slightly squeezing the index finger and thumb of the right hand. As you do the action, amplify the feelings flowing through you. Make the pictures more alive and vivid.

What we just did is called laying the anchor. When we recalled the event, we used our neurological components to cause an emotion to surface. The emotion has a name, like happiness or sadness. This is the linguistics component at work.

Linguistics, in this context, refers to our encoding and processing of a certain memory, which is not limited to just words. We further used the linguistics part by squeezing our fingers. The action creates a virtual bookmark in our minds. Now, our brains associate every squeeze of our fingers to a happy memory. Our reaction to the memory is our programing.

1. **Repeat**

TAKE a few minutes and do the action at least five more times. Make sure that your mind quickly associates the action with the happy memory you just anchored. With enough practice, a squeeze will quickly flash an image of happiness in your mind.

1. **Using the anchor**

BEFORE YOUR PERFORMANCE OR ACTIVITY, you can invoke the anchor to give you enough confidence to feel good and do well. When you use an anchor, amplify the feelings and then quickly break state when the memories are at their peak to maximize your performance. Cutting off the anchor moments before the peak will let the energy stay. Now open your eyes and you'll feel a surge of positive vibes. You can break state by doing something different, such as reading text messages or just looking at random objects around you.

CONTROLLING your emotions by collapsing anchors

Another application of anchoring is replacing negative emotions with positive ones. This is made possible by intentionally anchoring a negative memory and a positive memory, and then activating them both at the same time. At the end, the positive memory outweighs the negative one. Keep in mind, the more you practice, the more successful you'll become at this. This technique requires quite a bit of practice to master.

1. **Anchor the negative memory**

LIKE NORMAL ANCHORING, just recall a vivid negative experience. Make it real but not too overpowering or exaggerated, for that can make things worse. Use a gesture on the left hand to lay the anchor. Recall the anchor a few times just to make sure that you feel a negative state. Finally, break state for 30 seconds.

1. **Use a positive anchor**

NEXT, remember an experience that made you feel the opposite of the negative anchor. This is where you need to focus. Amplify the memory again. Meditate on the memory for another 30 seconds. Be sure to remember everything that happened. It is recommended to use an action on the right hand.

1. **Test the positive anchor**

WHENEVER YOU DO the action that recalls the positive anchor, make the mental picture balloon up. The feelings that correspond to this moment should also intensify. Let go of everything and allow the feelings to swallow you up.

Repeat this step 2-3 times then break state again for 30 seconds.

1. **Collapsing the anchors**

THIS IS the tricky part and will require practice. Keep in mind that the positive anchor must be more intense than the negative one. Breathe deep and relax. Once you are ready, activate both anchors at the same time. Don't worry if it feels weird at first, because your brain is just not used to feeling two contrasting emotions at the same time. Since the positive anchor is more intense, it will overpower the negative one and thus make it collapse. Once the positive state is in control, hold on to that state for another 10 seconds. Finally, open your eyes and you will feel a surge of positive energy.

MULTIPLE STATES by chaining anchors

The last technique showed you how to overpower a negative state by inducing a more intense one. This technique will teach you how to invoke several states in a short time, leading to an anchor with extreme amounts of positive energy. Chaining anchors can help if you want a surge of positive vibes taking over you, such as productivity, confidence, and relaxation. It is the most difficult technique but the one with the most benefits. Preparing for this method takes roughly 15 minutes.

1. **Preparing the chain**

ON PIECE OF PAPER, write down the current negative

state you want to change. Draw an arrow to the right towards the desired outcome.

A common example is: Stage fright → confidence

Once you have both the starting point and goal, it is now time to create the intermediate anchors. There are usually 2-3 intermediate anchors in between the current and desired states. The intermediate steps are the memories that will gradually lead towards your goal.

Next, list them all in order. Here is an example of a chain:

1. Stage fright before a performance

2. I get a feeling of disappointment because I don't have the courage to be confident

3. This builds my motivation to do my best so that everyone will be proud of my performance

4. I have rid myself of stage fright and I'm now ready to go.

The first stage is when you think about your current state. In this example, moments before your performance, you experience a case of stage fright. The second step is induced to move you away from the first one. It is a reason why you don't like your current state. After this, the third step creates a positive approach to overcome your problem that leads you to the realization of your desired outcome.

If you made your own chain, be sure that, as you go towards each state, there must be progression made from a negative state to a more positive one.

1. **Testing the chain**

NOW, lay the anchors by associating an action to each state. A common practice in chaining is using the fingers of one hand in a row. Induce the different anchors separately. This is to test whether the anchors can also work on their own. After each test, break state by doing something unrelated to what you're doing now.

1. **Using the chain**

FINALLY, you are ready to try the chain. Breathe deep and relax to prepare yourself. Recall the first state and focus. When you sense that the state is reaching its peak, quickly activate the succeeding state. Do this through all the stages. As you move on through the chain, make each mental picture even more vivid and alive than the last.

Once you reach the last stage, make the mental pictures as bright as you possibly can. Hold on to the feeling for at least 10 seconds once you reach the peak. Then quickly break state for you to maintain the energy from the exercise.

ANCHORING IS A VERY quick and effective means to move away from negative states. They require at most 15 minutes and are easy to learn. The more often the anchors are used, the quicker they can be applied to and positively impact your life. They are great to use before you perform or after you wake up.

4. **Get Healthy with NLP**

USING anchors to get motivated

Health programs are usually intensive and take months to finish. It's no surprise why many people quit just after a few sessions because they lose motivation. Being healthy requires sacrifices in lifestyle, and they are never easy to do.

Before getting started, make sure to anchor yourself in the right mindset by using the techniques discussed earlier. Some recommended states are determination, motivation, and patience. You can use either the basic, collapsing, or chaining anchors depending on your preference.

You can also use anchoring to remove feelings, such as cravings, by collapsing your state of hunger with the state of being full.

MODELING excellence

In any field, we all have people that we admire and look up to. We have high regards towards them because they show exemplary skill in what they do. Each of them has their own strategies for success.

Modeling is very similar to mentoring. It's using another person as an example for you to mimic. It involves putting yourself in the other person's shoes in order to gain insight and understand their thoughts and behaviors. After getting permission to model the person you admire, it is important to ask that person questions to identify his or her ways of thinking and behavior, and if you can't get in front of the person, you can use the internet (soon to be discussed).

It begins with carefully observing the subject and filtering for the strategies that they use in order to be successful (Druckman, 2004). For this exercise, we will use the example of losing weight. Modeling can also be applied in a variety of situations, including training for sports, public speaking, and parenting.

. . .

CHOOSE a subject

Using the weight loss example, think about a person that you think has an appearance similar to how you want to look. It's best to choose someone who has kept up that shape for a long time. A common subject could be an athlete because they generally practice good nutrition and utilize effective weight loss programs.

1. **Watch**

ONCE YOU HAVE A SUBJECT, research them. Focus on how they are able to trim down. There are a variety of internet sources like YouTube or Vimeo that you can use to search. Athletes often get interviewed on blogs and videos about their secret to keeping fit.

1. **Searching for the secret**

OBSERVE the behavior of the subject. Take note of how the health programs are executed. Also, look for certain characteristics that make the subject different from the rest.

- What type of language does he use?
- What are his beliefs?
- What does he value?
- What is his physiology?

You are finding the X factor of the person you're modeling. Reflect back and identify the defining characteristics that were present.

1. **After finding the X Factor**

ORGANIZE the information in a logical way that makes sense to you so that you can mimic or model it yourself. Test it out to make sure the desired results are achieved.

1. **Repeat**

REPEAT THIS EVERY DAY, or at least a few times a week. After applying this to your life for approximately 30 days, you or people around you will begin to notice positive changes in your behavior, attitude, and appearance.

5. **Attract More Wealth**

"IF YOU CAN IMAGINE IT, you can achieve it. If you can dream it, you can become it."

-William Arthur Ward

WEALTH IS a top priority for many people, so we will use money as the example of what we want to attract into our lives. Money is a sign of power and influence, and it also sends a message of hard work. It cannot buy happiness, but being broke or having no money can cause much stress, worry, and unhappiness.

There is a common misunderstanding of how we get money. People often tell us that to earn money requires going through numerous obstacles. This is not true; to get money, one of the most important strategies is the right mindset. **The Law of Attraction (LoA)** states that thinking positive thoughts can lead to those ideas becoming reality (Devilly, 2005).

Every thought releases a mental wavelength. The Law of Attraction heavily relies on the assumption that there is always an interaction between people and the universe. It can be inferred that even the universe has a consciousness. The message inside the wavelength represents our intent. Since the universe is interacting with us, it will receive the intent and also reply with the same thing. If you always wanted to have a promotion and you meditated that intent every day, the universe would most likely give you what you wanted. On the other hand, having negative or pessimistic ideas will give you unpleasant results. After all, being pessimistic creates doubt. And when we doubt, things are less likely to happen.

Napoleon Hill, the highly successful and widely recognized author, said that, "Whatever the mind can conceive and believe, it can achieve." In order for the Law of Attraction to work, we need to not only think it will happen, but also most importantly *believe* it will.

Here are a few steps you can implement today to make it happen:

1. Set up goals

WHEN WE MEDITATE USING LOA, our intent must be backed up with a clear and definite goal. Clearly defined outcomes make it easier to accomplish goals without feeling overwhelmed. "I want to be rich" isn't going to work. If you *do* want to get rich, then creating a path or steps that will lead to that goal is far more effective. An example could be, "By December 31st, I will have a startup business that will give me profit. To do so, I will dedicate three hours (4pm-7pm) every weekday to work on it." This is a place to start, and of course you want to get more specific. Ask yourself, "What will I specifically be working on during those hours?" and create specific deadlines to work towards your bigger goal.

Get a piece of paper and write down everything you want in your life. Narrow down this list to the most important to you.

Your goals are the heart of LoA. Do not generalize. Instead, be specific and create the steps to your desired outcome.

1. **Changing your belief system by reframing**

THE BIGGEST CHALLENGE to success is ourselves. On the back of the paper, list any limiting beliefs that might get in the way of achieving those goals (e.g., "I don't deserve it," "I'm not smart enough," "I can never lose weight," "I can't focus on one thing for more than a minute," or "I can never get anything right"). Be honest with yourself, for it is only with genuine intent that we can make things a reality.

These are our personal convictions about life that CAN be changed or shifted. Your goals will not come true if they are clashing with your own beliefs. As much as we want to reach success, a single cloud of doubt in our ability to achieve it can block us from achieving our goal.

Read the backside of the paper you just wrote. The challenges we wrote down are beliefs. Using the technique called framing, we can alter those negative thoughts and replace them with positive ones. Your unconscious mind cannot process a negative. It first interprets the thought as neutral or positive, and then with the "not" or other negative term, it attempts to flip it around.

An example of changing a negative statement to a positive could be instead of saying, "Don't be **afraid**," say, "Be **brave**." Notice the difference and impact between those two statements. If you are already doubting your belief, think of a time when you were brave because everyone has had moments in their life where they were either forced to be brave or chose to be brave. What about the first time you raised your hand to answer a question in class? Or the time you introduced yourself to someone new? Or the first time you asked someone out on a date? By stating what you *do* want, you increase its awareness, causing it to be more likely to happen.

To frame, you must first close your eyes and visualize yourself. Imagine yourself in a movie. You are the director and you dictate what happens in it. Think about your limitations or negative beliefs, and then reverse them. For example, "I can't lose weight," becomes "I CAN lose weight." or "I can't do anything right," becomes "I CAN do things right." Next, you must apply that belief in the "movie." Actually see yourself doing it and defying your own limiting beliefs. Play the movie as long as you want. You've just showed your mind that you can do better. Open your eyes and tell yourself that you can replicate what you saw in the mental movie.

Mentally playing the response you want in your mind will significantly increase the chances of it happening. Framing is useful in creating an alternative reality and then applying it in your own life.

1. **Meditate**

ONCE YOU'VE FRAMED yourself as being successful at what it is you want in life, then you genuinely believe you can achieve it—whether it's overcoming limiting beliefs or achieving goals.

Every morning, go to a quiet area, sit down, and take five to ten minutes to think about your specific goal and what you can do to get closer to it today. You can opt to use soft music to help you get into the right mood, or use a mantra to get you in a relaxed state of mind. Visualize money being around you. Motivate yourself to be productive and positive.

When we use LoA, we feel more confident that the goals we want are what we genuinely want. Your goals will also not come true the next day. It takes patience, determination, and consistent action for you to achieve them.

26

NLP in Business

Meta programs and chunking

Meta programs and chunking can be highly effective in business settings. They are essentially filters that determine how you view the world around you and have a huge impact on your behavior and how you communicate with others. The Meta Model is effective and helpful when attempting to understand another person's perspectives of the world–his beliefs, limiting beliefs, and choices (Corballis, 2012).

In NLP, you can either chunk up or chunk down. If you chunk up, you are looking at the bigger picture. Examples of questions to chunk up would be "What is this a part of?", "What's the bottom line?", or "What is the intention behind all this?"

Chunking down is taking something and looking at it from a detailed or more specific perspective. Examples of chunking down questions could be "If I were to cut this situation into slices, what would it look like?", "What are the specifics of this situation?", or "Can you give me an example?"

It is helpful in business settings and for negotiation purposes to either chunk up or chunk down until you and the other party can come to an agreement. This system allows each of you to come to a mutual understanding and bring in perspective shifts to match each other's level.

Just as with anything new, meta programs and chunking take consistent practice and can be highly effective once mastered.

ACCELERATED LEARNING

Learning takes place beyond the four corners of the school. Even after graduating, employees are continuously bombarded with loads of information that they have to read through. Especially in a competitive market, products and new technology elevate the playing field. These new innovations can alter your performance, both as a business or an employee. Learning new techniques will be easier if you apply accelerated learning strategies.

By using key concepts tied to NLP, accelerated learning strategies further maximizes the brain's potential to receive, process, and recall information in a snap.

Integrating accelerated learning in your business gives you numerous benefits. Compared to conventional training methods for new employees, accelerated training courses reduce training costs and length. It is even more effective in delivering information because courses under accelerated learning are learner-centered.

Aside from improving the capability of new employees, accelerated learning can also be augmented in the workplace, especially during meetings. Business meetings revolve around discussing heavy matter and a ton of information.

Often times, employees become detached from the

discussion when saturated with information, thus making the meetings unproductive. By using accelerated learning strategies, big information is effectively brought to the employees in bite-size pieces. Furthermore, these techniques arouse the interests of participants, and activities become interactive.

REPRESENTATIONAL SYSTEMS

Each person sees the world through the five senses: sight, hearing, touch, smell, and taste. We use these senses to learn, from walking to running. People learn most effectively when all senses are being stimulated and their preferred sense is targeted.

Furthermore, each person has a preferred learning method or representational system. In education, we have three main types of learners: visual, auditory, and kinesthetic. Visual learners prefer reading content off books and handouts. Auditory learners would rather sit down and listen to the discussion. Kinesthetic learners like hands-on activities.

Here is a quick test to assess your learner type:

LEARNER TYPE TEST

Choose the characteristic that best suits you.

CLASSROOM BEHAVIOR – Do you prefer:
 a.) Listening to the facilitator
 b.) Reading books and modules
 c.) learn through hands-on activities

. . .

SPEAKING BEHAVIOR – Do you:
- a.) Speak a lot
- b.) Speak seldom
- c.) Speak with a lot of gestures

MEMORY RECALL – Do you:
- a.) Remember what was discussed
- b.) Remember the visual aids
- c.) Remember the physical experiences

MOST LIKELY, if you answered:
- A in all questions, you are an auditory learner;
- B if you are a visual learner;
- C if you are a kinesthetic learner

SPEECH PATTERNS

Checking speech patterns is also an effective way to see a person's learning type. Engage with people and observe carefully the words they use. Watch out for clues that imply their learner type. Certain phrases like "I see your point" indicate a visual learner. "This rings a bell" is a sign of an auditory learner. "I think I got it" indicates a kinesthetic learner. These speaking patterns are also useful in finding out other people's learning type so you can adjust to their language to connect easier and more effectively.

Visual learners primarily use words like look, see, reveal, clear, etc.; auditory learners primarily use words like listen, harmonize, tell, squeak, etc.; whereas kinesthetic learners will use words like solid, grasp, catch on, tap into, etc. Often times our senses overlap, but we each have a primary one we prefer when it comes to learning and understanding the world (Masters, 1991).

Understanding how our minds work will make you realize how important it is to properly deliver information. The presentation of matter will decide whether a person will be receptive to it or not.

EYE ACCESSING CUES

When a person is speaking, you can use their eye movements to help determine whether a person is thinking using pictures, feelings, or sounds. This provides you with information on what their preferred learning style is.

The eyes will generally move left or right depending on what the subject's dominant side is. For example, if the person is right-handed and he is recalling a memory, he will look to the left; if he is creating something new or telling a lie, he will look to the right. If a person is describing something she's seen or imagining something new, she will look upward; if she is recalling something she's heard or creating something new, she will look laterally or to the side; if she is recalling how it felt or imagining how it would feel, she will look down (Bandler, 1975).

One way to start practicing could be observing people inside a coffee shop or watching characters on TV. Also, keep in mind that this is not always 100% correct, so if a person is right-handed and he's looking up and to the right, don't *always* assume that he is telling a lie.

SETTING the mood for learning

The venue of the activity plays a role in how receptive the person is to the information. According to research, facilitators must subliminally suggest the learning type of the participants to get them into the mood of learning.

In trainings for new employees, a good way to do this is by setting up posters and images that give the trainees a quick preview of things they are going to discuss. Also, giving a room light and color induces positive responses from the subjects. The mind needs to be stimulated in order for it to receive information quickly.

In boardroom meetings, you can lighten up the mood by removing all clutter or unnecessary objects that distract from what's important. Architects concluded that even the space of a boardroom can affect creativity. They recommend having a room that has light and plenty of space because it creates an atmosphere of freedom for the mind to learn. A small, cramped space, however, boxes the mind in and creates a feeling of being enclosed, thus making the participants uncomfortable.

BECOMING a good facilitator

Facilitators must not only be knowledgeable about the subject matter, they must also be approachable and positive. Being intimidating isn't healthy for a team to grow. A facilitator that lets each person speak his or her thoughts creates an environment conducive to learning. Other than that, facilitators need to be supportive. Positive reinforcement by encouraging a hesitant person to share their sentiments can improve the discussion. Usually, people who have ideas that are good have second thoughts before sharing them.

Afterword

Neurolinguistic Programming has the power to immediately change your thought patterns. It can take a perspective of "self doubt", and immediately transform it to one of competence and excellence. Once you have learned how to implement the strategies discussed throughout this book, your life will never be the same. Let's continue onto the next section and set some goals so that you can accomplish what you want in this life.

Section V. Set Goals to Reach Eternal Happiness

V. Section Set Goals to Reach Eternal Happiness

Introduction

You're here because you want to achieve something. You have a goal. So what is it? Is it to get out of bed today and feel excited about your day? Maybe it's to write a book that you've been putting off for way too long? Spend more time with your family? Rekindle lost relationships? Maybe run a half-marathon by the end of the year? Or drop 15 pounds? Or travel to Europe or Australia? Or maybe start a business that you love and are passionate about? Or get into an amazing relationship?

You've already taken the first step to making it happen—you've purchased this book because you are ready!

This section will guide you to accomplishing goals using the S.M.A.R.T. system and other powerful strategies to keep motivated and focused until you achieve your goal.

You will discover the 10 core steps to starting strong and reaching the finish line at full speed, thinking, "Wow, that was fun and easier than I thought!" There will be a simple and fun task for you to complete to bring you closer to accomplishing your goal. This section will give you the extra push to get it completed, and for people who do not know 100% what they want or how to get it, you will soon be staying motivated, focused, and *building* your life instead of sitting back and watching life pass you by!

Let's begin!

1. What are S.M.A.R.T. Goals?

The S.M.A.R.T. system is a way to accomplish tasks faster and easier and majorly increase your productivity. Successful CEOs, entrepreneurs, brainiacs, and people like you and me use the S.M.A.R.T. system to achieve goals. It is the backbone to success. I've read books and emulated people who have been successful in life, such as Richard Branson, Oprah Winfrey, and Steve Jobs. They all have one thing in common–they set S.M.A.R.T. goals, get into action, and along the way use strategies to keep the dream alive until it is achieved.

For example, Richard Branson's vision of creating the Virgin Galactic which can launch you to outer space, or Oprah Winfrey's vision of creating the Leadership Foundation Academy which is a free school for young girls in South Africa, and of course Steve Jobs who envisioned creating the Apple iPhone, iPad, and Apple HDTV were all dreams that became realities.

This system is rooted on the sole principle that life does not control us; instead, we are in control of our lives.

The good news is that this system can be used to complete almost any task. It takes a complicated process and breaks it down into simple, manageable pieces that line up like ducks in a row.

Welcome to the S.M.A.R.T. system, which stands for Specific, Measurable, Attainable, Realistic, and Timeline. Here's an example I used to successfully start a coaching business:

Introduction

- **Specific:** I will launch a life coaching business.

- **Measurable:** I will be sign up my first paying client within 2 weeks and give one sample coaching session a day (5 per week).

- **Attainable:** I will attend one networking event each day. There I will meet the speaker and two other people and get their contact information. I will follow up with these people the following day and offer them a sample coaching session. After each session I will find out if they want to continue coaching with me and offer them specific value they will receive from coaching with me.

- **Relevant:** Coaching people will allow me to make a positive impact in other people's lives and lead them to answers, which I am very passionate about.

- **Timeline:** Roots Coaching will have its first paying client in two weeks. By December 31st, I will have 10 coaching clients.

Jump in the S.M.A.R.T. way

As mentioned before, the S.M.A.R.T. system is an acronym that stands for Specific, Measurable, Attainable, Realistic, and Timeline. ALL five components are essential to success with the S.M.A.R.T system; failing to complete even one step will significantly reduce the chances of success. If you leave one out, it would be like building a table but forgetting to attach one of the legs.

One of the most rewarding things about having goals is

that you will wake up feeling more excited about your day, knowing that the days of your life are filled with a specific purpose.

Let's first take a look at some examples of how to utilize the S.M.A.R.T system with regard to career, health, and relationships.

Health

The gym is always flooded in January with people who have New Year's resolutions to lose 5, 10, 20 pounds, or get 6-pack abs. Then attendance begins to dwindle down month by month. This is because people either don't have a compelling enough reason to continue working out and lose motivation, or they get too busy and the resolution is soon forgotten about until next January.

You can use S.M.A.R.T. to stay on track and keep moving forward with your exercise regime and eating habits in order to lose weight and/or gain muscle. It can help you to find out if the regime you have chosen is working for you by applying the Specific and Measurable components.

For example, you could say, "I will lose between 1.5-2 pounds each week for six weeks," and then after a week goes by, you can look at your progress and see if you've lost 1.5-2lbs each week. If not, go back through your week and determine what you can cut out to improve *this* week– maybe cut out the late night junk food snacks or go to the gym 4 times instead of twice. This is also where a health journal can come handy for tracking the food you eat and exercise completed.

Love

The S.M.A.R.T rule can also be used in your love life. Finding love is important to all of us. To find love, you

Introduction

need to have a solid plan. In other words, it is ideal to imagine qualities that a potential love partner needs to have to be compatible. Be Specific about the top 3 qualities you want your love partner to have.

For example, you could say, "Connection, adventure, and intelligence," or "Funny, charming, and romantic." Then, as you meet people, learn about them and decide if that person has the top 3 qualities you're looking for. You can also do this for the top 3 qualities you do NOT want them to have. For example, "Negative, loud, or extremely jealous," or whatever qualities you don't like.

Then think about activities you enjoy doing. For example, if it's hiking, you could join a hiking club or hiking meetup group on www.meetup.com. Also, think of what your Timeline is when it comes to dating. For example, "I will have a girlfriend by March 1st (2 months away) and I will meet two new women 5 days a week."

Often love is not planned, and it is not known when Mr. or Miss Right will appear, but having a plan in place will increase the chances for success when you see someone that looks like a potential partner. So if this is what you want, create a plan, get into action, and make it happen.

With the S.M.A.R.T. planning process, you will be able to find someone you love faster while keeping yourself from wasting time on people you aren't likely to have a happy relationship with, minimizing the likelihood of encountering disappointments. The key is to be as specific as you can when it comes to finding someone to love.

Happiness

Finally, you can use this rule in order to increase happiness; for some, happiness is created from external factors, such as a financial reward or acquiring a beautiful home. Others get happiness from learning a new talent, taking a

Introduction

vacation, or moving to a new city and feeling at peace while listening to the waves crash against the rocks. Some want to have a luxury car, while others want to invent something. Writers want to create the perfect book, while athletes want to be stronger and more efficient in their respective sports.

Another note on happiness is that it is really easy to access, much easier than people make it out to be. It involves being in the present moment and enjoying *every* moment. You may be wondering how that is possible.

Step 1:

Before you start planning for your future, there are certain things that you need to establish. First, give yourself some time today to assess your life. Grab a piece of paper and go to a quiet spot in your home. Now, sit down in that quiet place and take a few deep breaths as you relax.

Take a look at the following categories and rank them each 1-10, with 1 meaning "nonexistent" and 10 being "the best!" Go ahead and rank your life today.

1. **Family and Friends**
2. **Health**
3. **Money**
4. **Career**
5. **Fun and Recreation**
6. **Significant Other/Romance**
7. **Physical Location**
8. **Personal Growth**

Look back over the categories. What do you want to change in each of these categories? What do you need to do to bring you closer to a 10? Take a second and imagine being there. What would it

Introduction

look like? You can say it aloud to yourself–I won't tell.

- Imagine your life if NOTHING changed, and it stayed at the same level 1 month, 6 months, and one year from now.
- How bad do you want this life you're imagining?
- Imagine tomorrow. What do you see?

Now that you have your list of areas that are strong and areas that you want to improve, you can use these ratings as a starting point and work to improve them. This will allow you to check in every so often (i.e., weekly, monthly, etc.) to see where improvements have been made. Let's keep moving forward!

27

How to Set an Unbreakable S.M.A.R.T. Goal!

WHY do you want to achieve your goal? What will it bring you? You must answer this question or stop reading. This answer will be one of your strongest motivators.

S IS for **SPECIFIC**

Your goal must be specific. The more specific your goal is, the greater chance at successfully accomplishing it. Take, for example, "I want to lose weight." But I say, "Ok, that's great! How much do you want to lose?"

"I want to lose 15 pounds." Clearly this is more specific.

Here are a few more examples of specific goals:

- I will earn a $100,000 per year in my online business.
- I will drive a brand new Mercedes S Class.
- I will buy a new house.
- I will be in a fun, healthy relationship with a

person I connect with, can have deep conversations with, and who is adventurous.

MAKE it observable

To ensure that your plan is specific, make it observable. Make it so that you can hear or see yourself doing it. A person should be able to see it. For example, you should see or imagine yourself driving a brand new Mercedes S Class, see yourself walking into your new house, or see the $100,000 on your bank statement.

THE ROADMAP

Of course, creating a plan to reach this goal is important. It's like a roadmap to your destination. You must start from point A and get to point B, but in between there could be traffic, detours, or stops that need to be made along the way. With a plan, you can organize all the necessary actions and establish a schedule for when things need to be accomplished to stay on track.

Otherwise, if you're always in the dark and you do not have a plan, you will surely not be able to get your goal by anything other than luck or chance, or you may achieve it but you might not even realize it.

With specific plans, every idea used will have a specified task. For example, if you want to make $1,000 more per month, make a list of things you need to accomplish to get there. If you're in sales, maybe you need to contact 15 new prospects per day instead of the usual 10. Maybe you need to set up 10 appointments per week instead of 8. Make out a schedule and set up specific times you will do this. For example, on MWF, I will make calls from 1-5pm with two 20-minute breaks, and on Tuesday and Thursday I will have appointments to meet with 5 people between 11am and 7pm. Again, it goes back to being as specific as possible.

If your goal is to lose 10 pounds, you could say, "To feel more attractive, I will lose 10 pounds in 3 months by joining a gym and working out MWF from 12pm-1pm," and so forth.

LANGUAGE

Another key point is to use language that appeals to you because the language can significantly change how you feel about your goal. Words produce emotion. They can excite you, or make you feel nothing at all. The objective should be to make the language as exciting and compelling as possible.

Here's an example: "I will easily drop 10 pounds of fat to feel more attractive, weighing 150 pounds at 13% body fat, while totally loving the process." Other words you can use might be "to have a sexy body" or "to have more energy." Whatever works for you so that you can feel energized and excited about your goal.

Step 2: Make your goal Specific. Look at the examples above, and make your goal specific enough so anyone can be clear on what it is *you want*.

M IS for MEASURABLE

The task of measuring something may seem super simple and easy, although it is usually the task people have the most difficulty with. If you don't measure it, how can you know when your goal is EVER met? And how can you make any changes if you make a mistake so that you do not keep going in circles?

Your goal needs to be something you can measure on a regular basis. Most people set their New Year's resolutions but fail to look at the progress or regression, leaving them incomplete and eventually forgotten. Another reason the goals need to be specific is because you can't measure "I want to earn more money" but you can measure "I want to make $1000 each week."

A measurable goal shows tangible evidence for any progress or regression. It can be used as an indicator that the goal has been achieved. Your goal must be something that you can measure regularly (e.g., weekly, bi-weekly). It is important to track progress and decide which, if any, changes need to be made.

Put it on your calendar, or set an alarm so that whenever it goes off you have to stop everything and take your measurements to see your progress. To maximize this process, you must have a way of measuring the goal consistently to see whether or not you're making progress. A weekly check-in or review is usually sufficient to determine what is working or if anything needs to be changed.

We need to measure to our progress to see results. It is hard to see changes from day to day because you are with yourself all day long. It's kind of like when you start working out for a few weeks and you don't feel like you look any different, then a friend says to you, "Have you been working out? You're looking good." You may not have noticed, but your friend did–that's the role that tracking your progress will play.

When you're seeing positive results, you'll be more motivated to keep working hard. Measuring your plans will let you know exactly when you have accomplished your goals, and then you can celebrate or reward yourself for your achievement.

Step 3: Make your S.M.A.R.T. goal Measurable. If your goal is to lose 15 pounds, when will you have it completed by? Can you break it down further? For example, "I will lose 15 pounds in 4 months." Then you could say, "Each week for the next six months I will lose 1 pound per week and will happily go to the gym three times a week to use the treadmill for 20 minutes and lift weights for 30 minutes."

A IS for ATTAINABLE

Your goal must be attainable. If you set up a goal that is impossible to attain, then you are setting yourself up for failure and will likely be disappointed in yourself. So, let's make it attainable.

You can attain almost any goal you set when you plan your steps wisely, establish a time frame that allows you to perform those steps, and make the goal compelling enough that it MUST get done.

STEP 4: Make your S.M.A.R.T. goal Attainable

A coach of mine taught me an easy and fun way to discover attainable goals. Here's what she recommended. First, take out a pen and paper and create a list of words that you believe about yourself, including your current skills and strengths. If this isn't easy to do, then you can ask a family member or a friend to name a few of your recognizable positive qualities.

Next, take a look at your goal and match the

qualities you'll need to bring to the table to reach your goal. You can base "what is Attainable" on your past achievements, such as any awards you were given or milestones at work.

Then, think of the qualities you have that will contribute to the process of the goal. For example, you could say, "Charm, education, and people/social skills." Keep that paper as a reminder of what skills you have and as something you can look at if you begin to doubt yourself or lose hope in your goal.

GOAL:
_____

MY QUALITIES that will contribute to achieving this:
1. _____
2. _____
3. _____
4. _____
5. _____

R IS for REALISTIC

Your goal must be realistic. How realistic are your plans? Are you planning to make $1,000,000 by next year? Or lose 5 pounds in a week? Or buy a $500,000 house if your income is only $40,000 per year? All of these are *possible*, but sometimes the hardest question is, "Are they realistic?"

If you want to earn $100,000 next month but you

don't have a job, that is not realistic. I encourage thinking big. However, if you set a goal that is too unrealistic so that even YOU don't believe that it can happen, it can have damaging effects, such as continuously letting yourself down. Instead of feeling gratified and accomplished, you could end up feeling worse about yourself than before.

In most cases, realistic plans will be tangible. You should be able to experience it through your senses, including taste, smell, sight, touch, and auditory.

CONSIDERATIONS

Dreams you have right now may be realistic if you work hard, plan ahead, and keep pushing even when times get tough. However, some of your dreams may not be financially possible at the moment, so make a plan to make it financially possible—if you want it bad enough—and set up a savings plan so you can save money towards it. Before you dive in to this goal, you must break it down and determine if that goal will work for you.

If your goal is to have perfect abs, you should set the right timeline so that your goal will be attainable. If you need more information on figuring out a realistic timeline, there are many health magazines that can guide you, or you can hire a personal trainer to show you strategies to reach your health goal.

The Attainable and Realistic rules complement each other. If your dreams are not attainable, then they might not be realistic. There are some things that can be realistic to some people and not to others. Be honest with yourself when considering if your goal is realistic for you.

For instance, if your goal is to spend more time with family instead of working so much, you are going to have to say "no" to a lot more things to make family time. If you know that you are not willing to *(or cannot spend less time at work)*, then it is not a realistic goal, unless you are willing to make other sacrifices (such as less sleep or less extra-curricular activities) to have more balance between work and family time.

If you need help deciding whether it's possible or not, consider asking a close friend or family member. Also, I recommend not asking anyone who is pessimistic by nature because they will likely shut your goal down completely. So, go ask a trustworthy, neutral to optimistic-minded person.

STEP 5: Make your S.M.A.R.T. goal Realistic
<u>Answer these Questions:</u>

- **Does it fit in your lifestyle?**
- **Do you have enough time to spend each week to make it a success?**
- **Do you have the financial means to begin?**
- **Do you have the knowledge or skills?**
- **Do you have the passion and perseverance to do what it takes to accomplish this?**

If the answer is "No" to these questions, then it's important to either modify or reconsider your goal.

T IS for Timeline

For a goal to be complete, it needs to be timely or have a timeline. A goal should be supported within a time frame. If there is no time frame, then there will be no sense of urgency. If you want to lose 10 lbs., when do you want to lose it by? "Someday" won't work, but if you place it within a time frame, like "by May 1st," then you've set your unconscious mind into motion to begin working on the goal.

Will you have a wall calendar or a flipbook calendar to mark your progress and remind yourself of deadlines? How about sticky notes all over your office or bedroom?

If your plan is based on a 10- to 20-year process, then you might have a hard time keeping your goal in mind and it will likely shift (which is okay). However, over time it might be difficult to keep pushing forward because it is so far out in the distance.

The solution to distant goals is to break them down into smaller pieces. If you have a goal to have 5 million dollars in your bank account in 10 years, then it needs to be broken down into smaller parts (e.g., a 5-year plan, a 1-year plan, a 1-month plan, and so forth). Time frames that are smaller, such as 1 week, 1 month, or even 1 year are much easier to see than 10 years down the road.

MAKE it urgent

Think about the power of a deadline. For instance, when you were in school there was pressure to complete an assignment or else there would be consequences—maybe after-school detention or a failing grade—requiring you to retake the course or even get expelled.

You want to create pressure on yourself to get it done. Create urgency.

Having consequences for not achieving a goal can be a strong motivator to get over the hurdles.

For example, if you don't complete your goal by your set deadline, what will you do that causes a bit of a sting?

Will you give $500 to your neighbor or a charity or a homeless man on the street? If you commit to this for each of your goals, imagine how many goals you will accomplish!

Step 6: Give your S.M.A.R.T. goal a Timeline and make it urgent!

What is a realistic timeline you can commit to for achieving your S.M.A.R.T. goal? Add a deadline (and urgency) to your goal, such as "I will lose 15 pounds in 4 months. If I do not, then I must donate $100 to a stranger behind me in Starbucks on (fill in a date)."

28

Why You (and Everyone Else in the World) Needs S.M.A.R.T. Goals!

Life can be chaotic, messy, and stressful. We can't deny that. Some days you may wake up thinking of all the things you need to accomplish and thinking there is NO WAY you can possibly get all of it done! Stress is created, and the important part is how you *choose* to use it.

Do you use it to energize yourself and get you going so you accomplish tasks at a more rapid pace than usual?

Or do you use the stress as a reason to mope, feel sorry for yourself, and stay in bed, getting very little accomplished? If you feel this way, here is a helpful strategy.

It is a perspective shift strategy. Answer the following questions:

- *Who is someone you admire?*
- *Examples could be a loved one (mom or dad), Richard Branson, Tony Robbins*

- *If that person were looking at you right now, what would he/she say for you to do?*

- *Use this as inspiration and motivation to get up and get busy!*

Habits

If your life is not the way you want it, it will stay that way until you consciously make the effort to change. Once you decide *what* you want, take small steps each day for 30 days until it becomes a habit and feels natural. For example, if you have a goal to lower your body fat percentage, you may have a plan to go to the gym every MWF and walk 2 miles on your off days. If you do this for 30 days, it'll become a habit. In fact, if you did this for 30 days, it'd feel strange if you didn't work out on those days, especially if you're seeing results–similar to the way it feels when you don't brush your teeth one night (or morning).

Other examples might include writing a book for 1 hour a day (which is how I wrote this book), or working on your business for an hour a day, or going to a coffee shop to meet 2 new people for an hour a day in order to network or find a new relationship–doing each for 30 days to form a habit.

Comfort zone

One of the hardest parts of reaching a goal is not only changing old habits, but also stepping outside of your comfort zone. Your comfort zone is where you feel most comfortable, but it brings only minimal rewards. Outside of your comfort zone is where you will find massive growth and reach your goals. It's fascinating to see what happens if you get uncomfortable and find out what you're capable of achieving.

For example, once I shifted my perspective using NLP, I finally gained the courage to talk to people who I thought were intimidating–the beautiful woman, the stiff professional, the wealthy boss. My life had completely changed. These people were on the same level as me, and now I felt comfortable and encouraged to talk with them.

After practicing shifting my perspectives with NLP techniques, I got my introverted self to be comfortable talking to anyone. After using these NLP strategies for several months, I saw a gorgeous girl sitting on a bench, and I had the courage and confidence to talk with her, the whole time thinking, "OMG, this girl is WAY out of my league, and she's talking to me!" Then, I got to know who she really was, and she became the most beautiful girl I'd ever met.

Ultimately, it is fear that is our worst enemy. What are you afraid of? Fear keeps people in their comfort zone, never attempting to reach for their goals. I know this because I did it for years. I was afraid of rejection, afraid of talking to people I'd never met and would probably never see again.

I encourage you to see what happens if you talk to that person in the coffee shop, or apply to that lucrative job, or take the leap to start a business that you're passionate about. If it doesn't work the first time, do it again, and maybe again until it happens. You'll notice that each time you do it, it becomes easier and more fun!

. . .

MANAGING your life

One of the most challenging parts to goal setting is finding the time to work toward it. Most likely, you are already extremely busy. That means you will have to say "no" to a few more things or cut back on something else in your life.

Think about the things you spend time on that really aren't necessary–Facebook, Instagram, Twitter, phone, texting, TV, YouTube. If you cut back 1 hour per day and used that hour to chase your goals, imagine where you would be in one month or one year.

24 HOURS, 60 minutes in 1 hour

Each of us is given the same amount of hours and minutes each day. The most significant factor separating people who win at goal setting and people who lose is how they spend their time.

- How do you spend your time?

BE curious about how and where your time is spent. Track it for a week. It is a good way for you to find out what you truly value in life.

LIFE IS NOT about waiting for the right time to come. It's about doing all the right things in the time that is given to you.

YOUR LIFE IS your creation

It is important to understand that everything you've

created in your life right now is something that you've set forth to get. Your life isn't an accident. You've focused your energy on something over a period of time and the things in your life were created, both the things you DO and DON'T want in your life. You must accept responsibility for *your* actions, which is one of the first steps to transforming your life.

You've created and manifested the job you love or hate, the amazing or awful relationship you're in, and the financial freedom or endless debt. You created it. If you can think it and believe in it, then you can create it. You and ONLY you can change your circumstances. *You* can change your mindset, pre-existing beliefs, or perspective for literally *any* situation.

As Rhonda Byrnes said in her widely recognized book *The Secret*, "Thoughts become things." Whatever you focus your energy and attention on will manifest in your life. This is one of the reasons it is so important to keep a positive mindset and use positive language.

It sometimes takes a boatload of effort to see the glass half full, especially when things haven't been going the way you want. But, when you think about it, there is always something positive or good that can be uncovered in every situation, and that is where your energy should be focused instead of on everything that went wrong.

I'm not saying to completely ignore the negative things, but instead don't worry or dwell on the "what ifs" because you can't change the past. You can only learn from your experiences so you can do better next time.

STEP 7: Get a calendar in order for you to schedule and commit to your goal. For example, from 6-8pm MWF, I will completely commit to meeting

new people to network with (or begin a relationship with)–nothing else; or from 7-8am M-F I will work on the new business I am creating.

MARK EACH DAY up until your goal deadline on your Timeline. For example, if you want your goal completed in 3 months, I recommend blocking out the times each day and marking what you need to do for each of those days in order to reach your goal.

29

Staying Fired Up About Your Goals!

Motivation and drive are necessary to complete a task. The reality is that every action is driven by motivation. You get up from the couch to get a glass of water to quench your thirst; you read this book because you're motivated to learn something new, to get more information, or to get motivated to achieve your goals.

One of the strongest motivators for the human race is wealth, in order to provide for yourself and your family. Others are motivated by personal achievements, such as Roger Bannister in 1954 who dreamed of crushing the 4-minute mile.

The S.M.A.R.T. system is a form of motivation, since you have discovered and answered all the questions included in this book. Review your answers to these questions on a regular basis. Some prefer daily, and others review them every two weeks to keep focused and motivated; some read them multiple times a day to keep up the momentum, or when they are feeling discouraged or want a reminder of why they are shooting for this goal in the first place. Figure out what works best for you and make it a routine or ritual to review them regularly.

TAKE care of yourself

One of the simplest, yet most forgotten or overlooked things when it comes to maximizing your chances of success is the importance of taking care of the goal maker–yourself. This is especially important if you are under additional stress.

A FEW QUICK NOTES:

REMEMBER TO BREATHE. Take a few deep breaths at least every hour to get more oxygen to your cells. It will help you feel better and more relaxed.

KEEP hydrated by drinking at least 6-8 cups of water each day.

KEEP HEALTHY SNACKS AROUND-RAISINS, carrots, celery sticks, pistachios, etc.

GET up and move around at least once an hour to get your blood flowing throughout your body.

MAKE time in your schedule for a recharge–20-min nap, meditation, or walk.

. . .

PERSEVERANCE

Michael Jordan, one of the most celebrated athletes in the world, knows all about perseverance. When Jordan was a sophomore in high school, he failed to make the basketball team. The coaches said he was too short to play basketball, at only 5'11" (1.80m).

Instead of giving up or feeling down about being "too short" and not making the basketball team, he turned it around and made it positive. Michael Jordan stated, "Whenever I was working out and got tired and figured I ought to stop, I'd close my eyes and see that list in the locker room without my name on it, and that usually got me going again."

Jordan didn't make excuses. His dream was to be the best on the court. With strong perseverance and refusal to quit, he practiced more than his peers, which led to him becoming one of the greatest basketball players of all time.

Grit

Psychologist Angela Lee Duckworth conducted an extensive research study and found that the highest predictor of a person's success is "grit"–the combination of "perseverance and passion for long-term goals." The willingness to fail and keep moving forward is what sets successful people apart from the rest.

Thomas Edison made over 1,000 light bulbs before inventing one that finally worked.

Walt Disney was fired from a newspaper company because the editor said he "lacked imagination and had no good ideas."

Albert Einstein didn't speak until age four and didn't read until age seven. His teachers labeled him "slow" and "mentally handicapped." But Einstein just had a different way of thinking. He later won the Nobel Prize in Physics.

Dr. Seuss's first book was thrown out by 27 different publishers before finally getting published. He's now the most popular children's book author ever.

The reason these people made it was because they kept pushing forward even when the tide was pushing against them. It is okay to fail. Just because you fail many times doesn't mean you're a failure. It just means that you've learned ways that do not work for you.

SELF-IMAGE

Our self-image controls our lives more than anything else. You are what you think you are. If you don't see yourself being successful, you won't be. You can't be it if you can't see it. Your life is limited to your vision. If you want to change your life, you must first change your vision of your life.

A well-known figure who envisioned himself becoming the highest paid movie star in Hollywood is a man by the name of Arnold Schwarzenegger. He was unknown to most people in 1976 when a newspaper reporter asked him, "Now that you've retired from bodybuilding, what do you plan to do next?" He answered very calmly and confidently, "I'm going to be the #1 movie star in Hollywood."

The reporter was shocked and amused by Schwarzenegger's response. It was hard to believe that a huge bodybuilder, who had no experience acting and spoke poor English with a strong Austrian accent, could ever be the #1 movie star in Hollywood!

The reporter asked him how he planned to make this dream come true, and Schwarzenegger stated, "I'll do it the same way I became the #1 body builder in the world. I first create a vision of who I want to be, then I start living like that person in my mind as if it were already true." That sounds almost too childish and too simple to be true, doesn't it? But it worked! Years later, Schwarzenegger became the highest paid movie star in Hollywood.

Take Schwarzenegger as an inspiration (or anyone you look up to) and think, "If he (or she) can do it, I CAN TOO, AND I WILL."

CONFIDENCE BUILDERS:

Self-confidence can play a role.

If you want to boost your confidence, here are some things you can do:

1. Start doing positive affirmations **every morning** before you start your day. Positive affirmations are telling yourself who you want to be and reminding yourself of the amazing qualities you already have–and the key word is **positive**, so keep all the words positive.

For example, you might want to read off a list or look in the mirror and say aloud, "I am confident in myself. I am optimistic. I am intelligent. People admire me, etc." Don't just say it, but really feel it and believe it. I remember when I first started this, I felt ridiculous, but after a week or so it became routine and I could feel my self-limiting beliefs begin to fade.

It has powerful effects on your subconscious, and soon you'll be the person you want to be. Now create the list of qualities you want to have.

1. Surround yourself with people who already have high confidence and model their behavior. Often times, the best way to learn is to observe and then imitate people. It's kind of like when you're playing a sport; although it may be intimidating, it is far better for you to play with people who are better than you because your learning curve will significantly increase.

STEP 8: Take a realistic view of yourself. Do you need to improve one of these qualities? If so, take some time to improve it. For instance, if you want to feel more confident, do positive affirmations for a few weeks. If you're satisfied where you are at, let's move forward.

30

The Master Plan to S.M.A.R.T. Goals

These are the most important questions to ask whenever setting a goal. Also, I've included a few of my own personal goals from 2013. You can use my examples as starting points, guidelines, or however is most helpful for you.

To set a S.M.A.R.T. goal, answer these questions:

*Why do I want this goal?

1. What is something I want to accomplish?
2. What is important about this?
3. Who will be involved in completing the task?
4. When will I start?
5. Where will it happen?
6. What are the requirements and constraints?
7. What are the action steps I need to take to get it done?
8. Why do I need to accomplish this certain task?
9. When do I want it completed?
10. What are the consequences of not completing it?

*Why do I want this goal? (Yes again. Answer, and solidify the answer.)

Once you have answered all these questions, your goal will be specific and you will be on track for it to be a S.M.A.R.T. and highly effective plan.

Here's an example: "I will lose 15 pounds by going to the gym for 1 hour every MWF and Sunday. At the gym, I'll do 30 minutes of cardio and then strength training for the other 30 minutes. Once every 2 weeks, I will check in to see the progress made and to see if any adjustments need to be made. If I do this, then I will feel better about myself and have more energy. If I do not do this, I will give $20 to my parents for each day I miss." And bam! That's it! That's a S.M.A.R.T. goal.

Here are a few examples of my goals that I posted on a bulletin board in my bedroom and office. I'd read them every morning before I started my day to remind myself of my S.M.A.R.T. goals and how important it is for me to achieve them.

1. I will easily have a thriving life-coaching business by 12.31.13 (15 clients, $----/session)

Why?

- To make an income so I can travel the world, eat where I want, and create a family someday!

- To not have to struggle and worry about how I will survive.

- To show others that I CAN do it!

- If I don't achieve it, I will have to find a shitty job that I don't like just to make money to survive!

How?

- Have fun at networking events, lead networking

events, & give speeches on goals, positivity, dating coaching, and being in the present moment.

*If I achieve this goal, I will go on a fun, relaxing vacation in Cabo for NYE.

*If I don't do this, I will donate $100 to a charity of my choice.

2. I will easily be part of the (_____) improvisation organization by 12.31.13

Why?

- To be admired and looked up to by my peers.
- To meet and form relationships with people I admire.
- To have better social skills.
- I love learning about people.

How?

- Interview by 7.31.14, display learned skills, share knowledge with students.

*If I don't do this, I will never be able to make money with all the hours I've spent practicing improv.

*When I achieve this goal, I will go on a $500 shopping spree.

*If I don't do this, I will donate $100 to a charity of my choice.

3. I will easily create an impressive introduction "Life Coach" video by 7.15.13

Why?

- I will impress myself, my friends, and family, and they can promote me too because it will be awesome!
- To show potential clients "in person" who they would be talking to, making them more comfortable and more likely to want to connect with me.

How?

- Make script by 7.9.14, film video by 7.15.14

* If I don't do this, I won't be taking my business to the next level and will always be making less money than I could have.

* When I achieve this goal, I will go to the movie theatre!

* If I don't do this, I will donate $100 to a charity of my choice.

4. I will easily have a fit, toned, attractive body by 9.30.13

Why?

- Because I don't want back pain.

- Because I like to look toned and fit.

- It shows others that I respect myself because I take care of my body.

- I will fit better in my clothes, making me look better.

How?

- Lift weights 3-5 X/week, cardio 30 min.

* If I don't do this, my back will hurt and I won't be as confident about my appearance.

* When I achieve this goal, I will sign up for a surfing lesson.

* If I don't do this, I will donate $100 to a charity of my choice.

STEP 9: First, answer the questions above and write your answers down, then keep them as a reminder of how you originally felt about your S.M.A.R.T. goal.

31

Final Secrets That Only Few Know!

- **A goal board (vision board) has proven to be a very effective strategy to making dreams reality.** It is simply a large bulletin board that has pictures of things people want to achieve in life, such as financial freedom, a dream home, or a dream car; what is included on it to make it a goal board is the numbers (such as the income you want to earn this month or this year), and specific steps you can read each morning before you start your day to make progress toward your goal.

Visualization is important when it comes to dreaming and reaching goals. It is an exhilarating feeling to relish the joy of seeing your bank account with a five million dollar balance. It gives you the energy and willpower to work diligently toward your goal.

The more you desire something, the more effort you'll put into reaching your goal. The more you visualize that your dream can come true, the more inspired you'll be to make it happen.

When it comes to goal setting, the mind and the body are most effective when they can work synergistically. The more you want it and the more clearly you can see it in your mind, the more your body is energized and wants to go out and do what the mind is envisioning.

- **Fake it until you make it**

I DON'T LIKE to say you have to lie to yourself, but in reality you do. You have to act like you've already achieved your goal, and not just *act* like it but actually *believe* it. Believe you have already gotten a raise so that you can actually feel what it feels like to receive the raise. Remember *that feeling* and how to access it because you can use that as a simple way to motivate you if you're feeling unmotivated.

- **Put a large dry-erase board on your wall or even several walls**. List your goals on it. Next to or below each goal would be a list of the tasks and the days they need to be completed by, and of course after it's completed, you can put a sweet little checkmark.

ONCE YOU PUT up the board, look at it every morning when you wake up and every evening before you go to sleep. This will allow you to constantly keep your goal toward the front of your mind. It's also a good reminder of how much progress you've made.

- **If you want something badly enough, think about it, and keep thinking about it multiple times throughout your day.** Again, this is because you're thoughts influence your actions, so the more you think about your goal, the more likely your actions will be synchronous with your thoughts.

ONE OF THE most powerful motivational stories is the story of Anthony Burgess, who's best known for *A Clockwork Orange*. He had a brain tumor and was told he would die within a year. He knew he had a battle on his hands. He barely had enough money to feed his family and had nothing to leave behind for his wife, Lynne, soon to be a widow.

Burgess had never been a professional novelist in the past, but he *always had thoughts of becoming a writer*. Since he'd been diagnosed with a brain tumor, these thought of ways to make money through writing books were constantly on his mind. He was determined to leave something behind, so he pursued writing. He did not have a clue whether or not his book would get published, but he still went for it, with the primary purpose of leaving money behind for his wife.

He stated, "It was January of 1960, and according to the prognosis, I had a winter and spring and summer to live through, and would die with the fall of the leaf."

During that time Burgess wrote energetically, finishing five and a half novels by the time the year was over. But, Burgess did not die. His cancer had gone into remission and then completely disappeared. In his long and full life as an author, he wrote over 70 books. Without the death sentence of one year, he may not have written at all.

Many of us are like Anthony Burgess, hiding our brilliance inside. If you only had one year to live, how would you live differently? What would you do?

- **If you are beginning to lose steam with your goal, remember the big picture.**
  Remember those questions you answered. Take a look at those and the answers.

FOR EXAMPLE, when I was getting my college degree I was required to take some courses I–for the lack of a better term–could not stand because the subject matter was so boring to me, and it was much harder to get things to click. It felt like going for a goal *without a purpose*, until I recalled the big picture–getting a college degree, which will allow me to have a job, which will allow me to have a house, where I would be able to raise a family.

So, the way to persevere when you are losing momentum is to constantly remind yourself of the big picture. "Ultimately, this (*fill in the blank*) will get me to (*this goal*)." You can even add this to your vision board (or picture on your desk or as your screen saver) if you want a silent reminder of your goal.

- **Positive affirmations**

POSITIVE AFFIRMATIONS ARE both confidence builders as well as very strong ways to stay motivated. They will allow you to become "your ideal self." I strongly suggest adding these to your daily routines to maximize your goal success.

• Powerful questions

ANSWER these questions and write your answers down:
1. What is important about this goal?
2. How will my life be different after I achieve this?
3. How will I feel once it is accomplished?
4. What will I miss out on if I don't accomplish my goal?
5. How will I feel if I don't pursue my goal?

Use your answers as a reminder for why you *need* to accomplish your goal.

• The power of positivity, the mind & success

THE MINDSET HAS a lot to do with how successful you'll be. You've probably heard someone say, "Be more positive," or "You're so negative!"

Which one stings more? "You're so negative!" does, although they say essentially the same thing. The difference is that one has a positive spin on it and the other is negative. If you swap the negative words in your vocabulary with positive ones, your subconscious mind will pick up on it, and you will begin to see things in a more positive light.

If you aren't already doing this, try it for at least 3 weeks. First, mark down how you feel overall, and in 3 weeks let me know how you feel. You can email me: matt@rootscoaching.com. And for some accountability, each time you use a negative word, put a $1 in a bucket.

Then, at the end of 3 weeks, donate the money to a charity of your choice. Or take on any other accountability technique that causes a little bit of a bite or sting.

- **Accountability**

HOLDING yourself accountable or having someone, such as a friend, family member, or even hiring a life coach to hold you accountable to your commitment is one of the most important components of achieving any goal. The example above of putting $1 in a bucket is an example of self-accountability; if you hired a coach, he or she could send you text reminders, calls, or whatever works best for you to get what you need accomplished.

You can also create a "contract" in order to hold yourself accountable. Be sure to make it S.M.A.R.T. and list the penalties if you do not abide by the terms. Give it to a friend to make sure you abide by it, and be sure to sign it as well.

I promise myself to maximize my effort to achieve the following goals by the listed deadline:

1.

_____

_____

2.

_____

_____

- **Reward yourself**

ONCE YOU ACHIEVE YOUR GOAL, no matter how big or small, be sure to reward yourself. Maybe your goal is to eat healthy six days a week. If you do that, then reward yourself with your favorite meal on the 7th day of the week. Maybe you have a goal of building a business, which might take years to build. When you accomplish that, go out and do something fun, or buy a car or an extravagant vacation. The point is to be sure to reward yourself for all the work you put in, for every milestone. Begin rewarding yourself by taking a moment to feel proud of yourself for reading this book.

ADJUST when needed

Remember that revising plans is a good thing. Be able to roll with the punches and, when something doesn't go as planned, be willing to adjust. There will always be unforeseen bumps in the road. Those little bumps in the road will inevitably be there, and they will often put a dent in your plans. If you're feeling discouraged, go back and read your goals and why you need to accomplish them, or spend some time viewing your vision board and feel how amazing it would be to have it accomplished.

Step 10: Commit to at least 3 of these motivators to keep yourself feeling strong about yourself and your goal until it is accomplished. Now, go make it happen!

by

Afterword

Remember that your dreams will only become a reality if you are determined enough to step outside of your comfort zone and challenge your self-limiting beliefs in order to create the life you desire.

I've learned over the past 5 years that whatever goal you might have, whatever you can dream of, you can achieve. There are no limits unless you put them on yourself.

Of course, it does not come at the drop of a hat or from complete luck, but instead with perseverance and commitment.

Epilogue

You've made it to the end, or the beginning, depending on how you want to look at it. My hope is that you have already begun to apply the strategies you've learned throughout this book in order to achieve a state of happiness.

As stated before, life is like a roller coaster and emotions will go up and down. Therefore, it is impossible to be permanently in a state of happiness. However, if you embrace each of the feelings you have such as sadness, excitement, fear, and joy, you will be riding the roller coaster of life, and fully experiencing it, as opposed to never getting on the roller coaster, and avoiding the emotions that enter your world.

Lastly, go out and enjoy life. It is short, but long enough for you to live a fulfilling life of your dreams. One that is full of joy, peace, fulfillment, purpose, and peace of mind.

MUCH LOVE,
    Matt Morris

Citations:

1. Lavretsky, H., Epel, E. S., Siddarth, P., Nazarian, N., Cyr, N. S., Khalsa, D. S., ... & Irwin, M. R. (2013). A pilot study of yogic meditation for family dementia caregivers with depressive symptoms: effects on mental health, cognition, and telomerase activity. *International journal of geriatric psychiatry*, *28*(1), 57-65.

2. Iso-Ahola SE, Dotson CO (2014) Psychological Momentum: Why Success Breeds Success. Review of General Psychology 18:19–33doi:10.1037/a0036406

3. Lim, D., Condon, P., & DeSteno, D. (2015). Mindfulness and compassion: an examination of mechanism and scalability. *PloS one*, *10*(2), e0118221.

4. Jacobs, T. L., Shaver, P. R., Epel, E. S., Zanesco, A. P., Aichele, S. R., Bridwell, D. A., ... & Saron, C. D. (2013). Self-reported mindfulness and cortisol during a Shamatha meditation retreat. *Health Psychology*, *32*(10), 1104.

5. Mrazek M. D., Franklin M. S., Phillips D., Baird B., Schooler J. (2013). Mindfulness training improves working memory and GRE performance while reducing mind-

Citations:

wandering. *Psychol. Sci.* 24, 776–781 10.1177/0956797612459659

6. Carlson, E. N. (2013). Overcoming the barriers to self-knowledge mindfulness as a path to seeing yourself as you really are. *Perspectives on Psychological Science*, *8*(2), 173-186.

7. Zangi, H. A., Mowinckel, P., Finset, A., Eriksson, L. R., Høystad, T. Ø., Lunde, A. K., & Hagen, K. B. (2012). A mindfulness-based group intervention to reduce psychological distress and fatigue in patients with inflammatory rheumatic joint diseases: a randomised controlled trial. *Annals of the rheumatic diseases*, *71*(6), 911-917.

8. Tang, Y. Y., Lu, Q., Fan, M., Yang, Y., & Posner, M. I. (2012). Mechanisms of white matter changes induced by meditation. *Proceedings of the National Academy of Sciences*, *109*(26), 10570-10574.

9. Hölzel, B. K., Lazar, S. W., Gard, T., Schuman-Olivier, Z., Vago, D. R., & Ott, U. (2011). How does mindfulness meditation work? Proposing mechanisms of action from a conceptual and neural perspective. *Perspectives on Psychological Science*, *6*(6), 537-559.

10. Black, David S. et al. "Mindfulness Meditation and Improvement in Sleep Quality and Daytime Impairment Among Older Adults With Sleep Disturbances: A Randomized Clinical Trial." *JAMA internal medicine* 175.4 (2015): 494–501.*PMC*. Web. 12 July 2015.

11. Raes, F., Griffith, J. W., Van der Gucht, K., & Williams, J. M. G. (2014). School-based prevention and reduction of depression in adolescents: A cluster-randomized controlled trial of a mindfulness group program. *Mindfulness*, *5*(5), 477-486.